Guides to Hidden Springs

MARK GIBBARD SSJE

Guides to Hidden Springs

A history of Christian spirituality through the
lives of some of its witnesses

SCM PRESS LTD

334 00562 0

First published 1979
by SCM Press Ltd
58 Bloomsbury Street, London WC1
Second impression 1980

Filmset in 'Monophoto' Ehrhardt 10 on 11 pt
and printed in Great Britain by
Richard Clay (The Chaucer Press) Ltd
Bungay, Suffolk

Contents

Preface

True prayer is response – response to God's love. It takes us time to become sure of this. Then gradually our response often takes on what I can only call a contemplative dimension. And indisputably it can bring new vigour and love into our lives. There is solid evidence for that.

These last few years I have met many people who are seeking for a deeper life of prayer. Some have been influenced by renewal movements in the churches, some by various approaches to meditation and contemplation, while others have felt a genuine dissatisfaction with their own rather conventional prayers.

Genuine prayer calls for sustained effort. I have discovered this in my own attempts to pray. At times I have felt discouraged on this journey of prayer; but I would like to share with you the experience of men and women who have given me the help I so much needed.

These guides to prayer span the centuries and cultures. They come from the Nile valley of the Desert Fathers to the Paris of Louis XIII, from an American college to an Indian ashram. I can only sketch them, and I hope you will look into their letters and writings for yourself.

Real prayer does not mean running away from life; quite the contrary. It produced in Thomas Merton, contemplative as he was, a concern for social justice. 'Contemplation is the spring,' he wrote, 'action the stream.'

This fact came home to me again while talking to Mother Teresa in the slums of Calcutta. Everyone knows how thirty years ago she went out with only five rupees in her purse, to give her life to the poorest of the poor. And there she still is. Never shall I forget her words to me – though from other lips they might have sounded banal: 'This sort of loving comes only through prayer.'

Oxford
December 1978

MARK GIBBARD

I

John Cassian and the Desert

'It is more humanly beautiful to risk failure seeking for the hidden springs,' Theodore Roszak has written from the California State university, 'than to resign to the futurelessness of the wasteland. For the springs are there to be found.'[1] I should not have put it quite in those words; but what Roszak is writing about I have seen for myself in many countries.

People are putting a question mark against our conventional, materialistic society, and are looking for 'an alternative culture'. It is much the same with religion. Some of our churches are dwindling and perhaps dying; and where churches are alive, there is a searching for a new and deeper prayer. And in far wider circles these hidden springs are also being discovered.

The fourth century, the age of the Desert Fathers and John Cassian, was in some ways like our own. Around the Mediterranean came an 'awakening' which may be illuminating for us and perhaps encouraging. It was a reaction against the growing worldliness of the church.

When the Emperor Constantine in 313 ended the long persecution of the Christians, it became popular for men and women of that tired, pagan Roman society to turn to the church. With them came their wealth and so more splendid church buildings. Etheria, the Spanish pilgrim, wrote of the jewels in the new basilicas in the Holy Land; they were exceptional, but the trend was almost everywhere the same. Bishops were given secular privileges and responsibilities. To become a bishop of any sizeable city was now something worth coveting. Praetextatus, the pagan governor of Rome, said jestingly, 'Make me Bishop of Rome and I will turn Christian today.' Jerome, admittedly a satirist, could from his monastic retreat in Bethlehem describe clergy in Rome as men-on-the-make, stylishly dressed and always in-the-know. Churchgoing became as fashionable as in the

9

England of Edward VII. Crowds poured in, less than half-converted.

Some Christians could stand it no longer; they had to get right away from it. In protest they left for the wildernesses of Syria, of Palestine and above all of Egypt. I remember when I was in Egypt I was struck by how soon you are out of the narrow Nile valley into the lonely, sun-baked desert; and in that climate it is not too difficult to 'drop out' and live rough.

They lived in small clusters of cells. They plaited baskets and did other simple handwork. They were within reach of a more experienced hermit. 'Give me a word, Father,' they would say to him; and, reflecting on some pregnant phrase, would return to meditate and pray in solitude. Only on Saturdays and Sundays did they all meet together for worship.

The trickle of these hermits soon became a flood-tide. They were sincere, heroic men, though sometimes inhuman in their asceticism and competitively bizarre. One hermit set fire to a bundle of fifteen years' letters from his family without looking at them. Another used to carry with him 300 pebbles in a bag so as to count his 300 prayers each day; and was upset when he heard of a nun who said 700 prayers a day – and that in spite of the fact that she fasted five days a week! Idiosyncratic they were, yet their lives shone with an other-worldly charity.

Today in the desert of Wadi Latrun, Matthew the Poor and fifty Coptic monks are rebuilding the monastery of St Makarios and making a patch of desert blossom as a rose. You can see pilgrims coming again from Cairo, seeking inspiration and a spiritual guide.

As a genuine searcher John Cassian was determined to live among these Desert Fathers, not to be put off by their eccentricities, but to listen to their sayings, record them, sift them, and bring away for others a harvest of spiritual wisdom.

He went with his friend Germanus first to a monastery at Bethlehem. After a time they were given permission to pay a short visit to the more severe hermits of Egypt. And these two young men, as we might expect, overstayed their leave. 'What are we to do now?' they asked a hermit. 'Shall we go back to Bethlehem and keep our word, or stay on with you all and gain more spiritually?' The hermit thought for a moment and then came up with a biblical precedent; it may sound very odd to us today. 'At the Last Supper,' he reflected, 'Peter at first said to Jesus, "You shall never wash my feet," and then changed his mind, for his own greater benefit.'

Then the hermit concluded, 'So you stay here, in good conscience.' The Desert Fathers often reasoned in this ingenious sort of way; but you will find them also full of humour and of piercing insight.

Cassian and Germanus stayed on. They learned from simple Coptic monks. They listened to the austere Evagrius of Pontus and his disciples – Greek-speaking students of spirituality who had fled from the wasteland of their own civilization. But even the desert was no paradise. The Copts resented intellectual foreigners. Once, when Evagrius was speaking, a Copt interrupted him: 'Well, Father, doubtless you would be a bishop if you were at home; you would be at the head of things, but here you're only a foreigner.' Evagrius was dumbfounded. He died not long afterwards. The movement against these intellectuals intensified. They were driven out of Egypt, and Cassian and Germanus too.

The young men fled to Constantinople, where they were welcomed by Bishop John Chrysostom. But the bishop angered the Empress Eudoxia and others in that imperial city, and so was banished. Then Cassian travelled to Rome and became a friend of the future Pope Leo I. And when the barbarians were about to attack Rome, Cassian went on to Marseilles in one of the few pockets of peace in that threatened civilization. There in about 420 he founded two monastic houses and wrote two ponderous volumes, the *Institutes* and the *Conferences*, about the Desert Fathers. We too can enjoy hearing anecdotes about them, often as crisp as the sayings of Zen masters, in an anonymous collection of *Sayings of the Fathers*. They stand before us so vividly – clearly the same men – in all these records.

Strangely enough these hermits hit on what seem to me our three basic needs, whether we are just setting out on this journey or making a new start; the need for a persistent effort, the need for an aim as clear as possible and the need for guides to encourage us.

First, the life of each hermit unforgettably says to us – Without sustained effort, no true prayer. We have mistakenly tamed prayer too often in our churches. For Cassian prayer is a warfare against indolence and evil. So it is in the gospels. But never should it be a struggle in which we feel lonely; for, Cassian says, 'God no sooner sees in us the beginning of a good will than he at once enlightens, strengthens and exalts it to salvation.'

But if real prayer is a bit of a haul, how can we encourage someone only just starting or restarting? Let me elaborate this a little. It is so important. I remember how I began Hebrew: a totally unfamiliar script had to be read backwards; and masses of grammatical rules had then to be mastered without any obvious usefulness. Several times I nearly threw my Hebrew book out of the window. How glad I am now that I didn't, for Hebrew has given me the 'feel' of the Old Testament, which probably could not have come in any other way.

Mastering a new instrument also needs persistence. A friend of mine again and again nearly gave up learning to play the violin. It took years. Now it has brought immense pleasure to him – and to many others.

Something even closer to prayer is the building up of a deeper partnership between two friends. They need time and patience. They sometimes have gradually to work through personal difficulties. At first they couldn't have known what joys were in store for them.

So a beginner at prayer or at anything else can't possibly grasp right at the start the full value of what he is doing; but longer experience shows – and I hope this book gives some of the evidence – that authentic prayer can bring a new dimension into our everyday lives and become a fresh spring of caring and loving.

Secondly, we need as clear an aim as possible. Without this, Cassian tells us, we are like desert travellers 'who miss their way, but are still tiring themselves out, though they are walking no nearer to their destination'. The primary aim of prayer is, he underlines, the coming of the kingdom of God. For true prayer links the practical problems of life to God and his kingdom. Cassian in the desert sees this less clearly than the New Testament does or the psalmists. But without this concrete emphasis prayer narrows itself down to our personal link to God. Essential as our relationship to God is, Cassian calls it our secondary aim. And though deeply ascetic, he tells us that we shall not come to this I–thou relationship with God through self-denial in itself, but only through actions inspired by love.

Thirdly, Cassian stresses our need for a spiritual guide. True, we each have to make our own journey. But we can gain from others' experience – and avoid their mistakes. You will notice again and again in this book that we have also to translate into a contemporary idiom what others have written. Cassian himself has adjusted the extreme asceticism of Egypt to fit the colder climate of Gaul. One quality of a true guide is this kind of wisdom; and the Desert Fathers themselves say that without discretion fasting and solitude may do a man more harm than good. Cassian quotes the legend about St John the Evangelist stroking a partridge. A hunter saw him doing this and asked why so great a saint wasted his time in this way. John replied, 'And why don't you carry your bow always bent, with the string always taut?' 'If I did so,' answered the hunter, 'my bow would lose its resilience and strength.' 'So would my mind,' concluded John, 'unless I had this relaxation.'

In this book you will find, I hope, some suitable guides. But that may not be enough for all of us. As Bishop Theophan, an Eastern Orthodox guide of the last century, said, 'A book cannot provide all the detailed advice which is supplied by the *staretz* who understands the inner state which should accompany prayer.'[2] Perhaps we are too close to ourselves to advise ourselves. Our guide needs to be readily available.

I would like now to share with you a little of what Cassian picked up about prayer. He writes a great deal about vocal prayer, what we should call 'saying our prayers', singing the psalms and worshipping together. He implies that, even if some of us now are looking for a quieter, more contemplative kind of prayer, yet we shall never out-grow the need for these basic vocal prayers.

But he has much more to say about this contemplative praying of the Desert Fathers. Today ordinary men and women living in all the pressures of the world are discovering how it can enrich their lives. Yet not until the seventeenth century, in fact, was it appreciated that no one group had a monopoly of contemplative praying. And Francis de Sales, as we shall see, was about the first to point this out.

The way towards this particular kind of prayer is what Cassian calls in a wide sense 'purity of heart'. This doesn't mean that we must be 'cold' and without deep feelings, but that we must not be self-seeking and grasping; we should rather be moved by that quality of loving which we see in Jesus. When this quiet prayer comes to us, we experience it as a gift. It will sometimes, says Cassian, spring up from within us 'like some incomprehensible and all-devouring flame'. Some verse of a psalm or the sound of singing may set it off; or, Cassian adds, it may be given us when we are considering the sound of the sea, the waves, drops of rain, God's endless mercies and above all the Lord's coming for our sake into this life.

Then Cassian wishes us to find out how to continue to live in the spirit of this quiet prayer all through the day. This comes, he says, through daily meditation on the scriptures; he doesn't mean primarily an intellectual exercise, but a quiet pondering in the heart. And often during the day we should turn to God in a short phrase of prayer. His advice reminds us of the well-known repeated 'Jesus prayer' of the Eastern Orthodox. Cassian himself frequently uses a verse from the psalms – 'O God, make speed to save us: O Lord, make haste to help us.' He quaintly compares it to a spiritual hedgehog, whose spikes will drive evil away. So he recommends: 'Whatever work or ministry or journey you are undertaking, go on praying these words. Sleep ought to catch you thinking about this verse. When you wake, it should be your first thought and it should send you out on your daily work, always to be there with you.'

This frequent prayer like quiet, steady breathing can keep us continually open to receive God's love and so to transmit love to those around us. This is the secret of the charming kindnesses of the Desert Fathers. They were ready to break their discipline of fasting or of praying to welcome, listen to and encourage a pilgrim who came to them. When Cassian and Germanus called on a hermit, he even gave them his own cell; and the next day started to build another with his own hands.

These men left their world to learn prayer and love in the narrow, hard, demanding school of the desert – to us perhaps an irrational, almost an incomprehensible sacrifice. But mysteriously they were being trained to bring back a deeper prayer and a more generous love to our own world, the world to be born after the Dark Ages.

It was Cassian's books about the Desert Fathers that inspired the great Benedict. In his Rule he quoted them over a hundred times; he reaffirmed their teaching on personal prayer; and he recommended them for reading in his monasteries every evening.

And when in the next centuries the barbarians had overrun Europe, it was largely these monks that kept the heart of the church's praise and prayer steadily beating – and they still do now across the world. I think of St John's Abbey standing in its own college campus deep in the snows of Minnesota; and the Abbey of Maria Laach with its music and devotion, its learning and ecumenism in Rhineland; and the simple Priory of Mahitsy on its hill with a communal farm in Madagascar and its church ringing with marvellous Malagasy melodies. How often have I thanked God with all my heart for Cassian – when I have like so many others found myself strengthened and encouraged by worship in monastic churches like these!

The Desert Fathers sowed, and we in so many ways are still harvesting. For it was those earlier monks who in time brought to Christ the barbarian new masters of Europe. And it was chiefly through their monasteries that the learning of ancient Greece and Rome was preserved and merged into the yet richer culture of the Middle Ages. We shall meet this in Mother Julian of Norwich. But first we turn to its foundation in the scriptures.

2

Psalmists and being Ourselves

Cassian tells us how much the Desert Fathers loved the psalms in their solitude and in their worshipping together. Jerome wrote from the Holy Land about the same time: 'Wherever you turn, the ploughman with his hand on the plough sings Alleluia, the perspiring reaper diverts himself with psalms; and the vinedresser sings the songs of David while he trims the vine with his curved knife. These are the ballads of the country; these are, they say, its love songs'. (*Letter* 46. 12). Since then monasteries all down the centuries have echoed with the music of the psalms, and so have churches, Catholic and Orthodox, Anglican and Protestant.

Yet in our twentieth-century search for the heart of prayer, what do these ancient psalmists tell us? I can't speak for other people. But let me say clearly and briefly that above all else the psalmists tell me that in my praying I shall always need three things: frankness about myself, realism about my surroundings and a readiness to be changed. If the Desert Fathers tell me how to start the journey of prayer, the psalmists show me how to carry on.

For prayer to become real prayer, the psalmists show us how we must put into it our actual selves – as we are – our good points, as they seem to us, and our failings, our expectations and anxieties, our dilemmas and resentments.

'Lord, why don't you drop a thunderbolt on all that rabble?', says Don Camillo, the little Italian priest created by the novelist Giovanni Guareschi, talking to Christ about Peppone, the Communist mayor, and his party-members. An odd prayer, but far more genuine and therefore in many ways better than much conventional praying. The psalmists also pour out their anger before God: 'I hate them with a perfect hate' (Ps. 139.22) – and even their own complacency: 'As for me, I walk the path of perfection' (Ps. 26.11).

It is easy for us – and so disastrous – to try to hide our actual selves from God, whether we are saying traditional prayers or trying to be spontaneous. Of course we can't hoodwink God; he knows. But it is essential for us to open ourselves frankly to him. So it is better to blurt out our complaints to our Father rather than let them smoulder on in inner resentment. Better, too, to ask for whatever we think we need. Need and asking are so essential to our human nature that any minimizing it, let alone suppressing it, cripples our personality. And one of our fundamental needs is to know that we are loved. Without that openness, even God can't build up a living, authentic relationship with us. Isn't it the same if we want real relationships with our close friends? But neither in friendship nor in prayer is it always easy – yet we discover eventually how very worth while it is.

The psalmists speak realistically with God, not only about themselves, but also about the total setting of their lives; about kings and enemies, about priests and merchants, about prosperous families and a nation ruined. We too should *speak out* to God about our own situation. We don't try to dictate to him, but we tell him how we see the world and our lives; we acknowledge our limited vision, and we offer our desires and energies ready to be used. Only so can our prayer be real.

We can't expect over-simplified answers to our problems in prayer or in daily life either. But we can trust God gradually to inspire us to transform our petitions, and then our hearts and minds will also be transformed by God in the service of his kingdom. One of the psalmists had this experience in his prayer:

> I strove to fathom this problem,
> too hard for my mind to understand,
> until I went into the sanctuary of God (Ps. 73.16).

So I must learn to put my actual self and situation into my prayer, but then to be prepared to have myself changed – and my attitude and perhaps the situation as well. Being ourselves, we can become our true selves. This is, as I have said, the supremely important thing the psalmists have to say to me.

There are so many other good things in the psalms – indeed treasures, if we can learn to appreciate them. For example, the psalmists write marvellous lines to express their love and longing for God. I have copied out my own selection of them for my personal prayers. One psalm begins:

> O God, you are my God, for you I long; for you my soul is
> thirsting.
> My body pines for you – like a dry, weary land without water
> (Ps. 63.1).

I grant that sometimes these words may seem pitched spiritually a
bit too high for us. There are days when we can't genuinely say that
we love God like that – though perhaps we wish we did.

But isn't it like this also in human affection? If we express what
little love we have – sometimes in words which may sound slightly
beyond us – it often has the effect of making that love grow stronger.
Many of us want to respond to God, to love him more, whatever our
intellectual or other dilemmas may be; and I have found that these
lines, if I use them as sincerely as I can, really help me to grow in
love for God.

Then the stanzas of praise to God both for his creation and also
for his providential love are among the highlights of the psalms.
Indeed the Hebrew title for the 'psalms', *tehillim*, means precisely
'songs of praise'. Again and again the wonders of God's creation
evoke praise from the psalmists:

> To him belongs the sea, for he made it: and the dry land shaped
> by his hands.
> Come, let us bow and bend low: let us kneel before the God who
> made us (Ps. 95.5–6).

These lines awaken an echo in many of us – but perhaps not in all
who have to live in the pollution and tensions of an 'inner city'. And
even the language itself is a difficulty to some modern people;
'Come, let us bow and bend low'. It sounds to them obsequious
flattery. But God never courts flattery. He wishes us to express our
wonder and gratitude, rather, because this is essential to our human
nature; for, as William of St Thierry said, 'A man who has lost his
sense of wonder is a man dead.'

Again, isn't it the same with our human relationships? Though
we must start where we are and be genuine, yet don't words of
growing appreciation and wonder freshen and deepen our friendships and family ties?

So to use words of praise slowly and as deeply as we can helps
us to grow in fellowship with God and so into our true maturity.

Praise him, sun and moon; praise him, shining stars.
Praise him, highest heavens; and the waters above the heavens.
Young men and maidens; old men together with children,
Let them praise the name of the Lord (Ps. 148.3, 12).

Augustine, commenting on the psalms, prayed, 'Let no day go by in which I do not praise you, Lord.'

The psalmists also praise God for his providential love. One of them looking back over his life thanks God:

> I will declare the Lord's mighty deeds,
> Proclaiming your righteousness,
> O God, you have taught me from my youth,
> And I proclaim your wonders still (Ps. 71.14–15).

Full of praise is Psalm 107 with its glad refrain:

> Let me praise the Lord for his goodness,
> For the wonders he does for men.

I myself find it helpful to learn such lines by heart and to incorporate them into my personal thanksgivings to God.

We have often spoiled the psalms by our prosy literalism and caused ourselves unnecessary difficulties. The psalms are not theological prose, they are poetry, and Thomas Merton has written of them, 'A good poem induces an experience that could not be produced by any other combination of words.'[1] How can we share these experiences when we take the book of psalms into our hands? One difficulty may be the old translation. We may be understandably attached to it, as we are to the equally old language of Shakespeare. Yet it may obscure for us the essentially poetic nature of the psalms. It is not just a new translation we need, but a fresh one.

Poetry is hard to translate. But Dante has been translated. Scholars differ about Hebrew poetry, but they are all agreed that it has quite a simple structure. It has no rhyme, although it has assonance; it is built up of short phrases with light accent-beats; it is full of vivid, concrete pictures. All through the psalms we listen to the lines in parallel, reaffirming one another –

> Your word is a lamp for my steps,
> And a light for my path (Ps. 119.105)

– or sometimes supplementing or clashing with one another. Even the dullest translation can't conceal this. Some of us haven't time for very large commentaries. What most of us need, I guess, is a lively translation which keeps the 'feel' of poetry and also gives some lines of introduction to each psalm. The Fount paperback, *The Psalms*, a stimulating translation based on the Jerusalem Bible, seems to me to do both; and Professor H. H. Rowley has called it 'a very impressive rendering'.

The land of the psalmists, about the size of Wales, was on the whole a stony land; droughts were frequent, and the wilderness never far off. Only three monarchs ruled over the whole land – Saul, David, by tradition the first psalmist, and his son Solomon. Then it broke into two kingdoms, until one after the other was swallowed up by the empires of Assyria and Babylon. But over more than 400 years their kings had stood for a great deal more than modern kings do – and especially in the royal temple city of Jerusalem. How often have I sat on the Mount of Olives, looking across the Kedron valley at the temple area and picturing the crowds of families climbing that opposite hill with a psalm on their lips:

I rejoiced when I heard them say, 'Let us go to God's house.'
And our feet are standing – within your gates, O Jerusalem
(Ps. 122.1–2).

Mowinckel, the Scandinavian scholar, believed that each new year at the temple there was a great enthronement festival, the king in some way impersonating God. Whether that was so or not, the psalms capture the magnificence of the worship at the temple:

The Lord is king; the peoples tremble.
He is throned on the cherubim; the earth quakes.
The Lord is great in Zion (Ps. 99.1).

Then came the crash in 586 BC, the temple was in flames, Jerusalem flattened and most of the people deported. One of the few psalms which we can date with certainty expresses their homesickness: 'By the rivers of Babylon, there we sat and wept' (Ps. 137.1) – and also their anger. After seventy years some returned, but now to form a church rather than a nation.

It is a pity we often don't notice the variety in the psalms. For they were being compiled probably over a span of 800 years from David's time or even earlier. While some are personal prayers, many were written to be sung on great occasions. Dietrich Bonhoeffer wrote from his prison cell: 'I know and love the psalms more than any other book'; and he said he could not read some of the psalms without hearing the musical setting of Heinrich Schütz, and this association he called 'one of the greatest enrichments of my life'.[2]

At a recent international gathering at Abu Ghosh in the Holy Land we were all amazed at the spiritual variety and emotional force in a disc of psalms sung by King's College choir at Cambridge. Clearly much can be done by the use of imaginative musical settings to bring out the range of the psalms and to make them come alive for us.

But how are we to approach these poem-prayers of a bygone age that have so much to tell us? To begin with we need to read and re-read the psalms like other poems. We should start with those which really speak to us. If you don't know quite where to begin, might I suggest Psalms 67, 100, 103, 121 and 122? Then gradually extend your repertoire. Don't worry if at first you can't see what some psalm is all about. Coleridge used to say, 'Poetry gives most pleasure when only generally and not perfectly understood.'

It is often useful to start with the 'feel' of the land of the psalmists and its turbulent times. But then remember that all literature from Homer onwards has been re-interpreted by successive generations and so has acquired rich overtones. So don't hesitate to build your own overtones into the psalms. For example, I sometimes slip into my rucksack a small copy of the psalms, when I am in the mountains, as I do often a book of verse; and I jot down words in the margin – at Psalm 104 I have written, 'Great Gable, Cumberland'. Then I can relive the experience of that sunny day as I pray this psalm in my room on a foggy winter evening. I have made other links. I like to say Psalms 63 and 95 when getting up; and 31.1–6 and 134 on going to bed; and 84 when preparing for holy communion; and others, when interceding for my friends. So the psalms become part of ourselves.

You may feel able before long to share your insights on a psalm with a friend or a group of friends. This is a valuable step. For psalms are not only to help us to pray personally, but also to pray and praise God together; and for this we need to build also the church's overtones into the psalms.

We can hardly pick up the psalms without thinking of Jesus praying them in solitude and with his friends, in synagogues and in the temple. These psalms became so much part of himself, it seems, that words from them came spontaneously to his lips as he was dying on the cross.

The later Hebrews had already radically re-thought some verses in the psalms, originally about their past kings, and had projected them into the future on to some longed-for Messiah:

The Lord's revelation to my Master:
Sit on my right; I will put your foes beneath your feet
    (Ps. 110.1).

This hope Jesus in Mark's gospel sees fulfilled in himself. Also in Luke's story of Jesus' country walk from Jerusalem to Emmaus on Easter afternoon he said to his two friends, 'Everything written about me in the Law of Moses and in the prophets and psalms was bound to be fulfilled.'

It was on this basis that Bonhoeffer, radical theologian though he was, encouraged his students, the future pastors of the Confessing Church in the Hitler years, daily to use the psalms as 'the prayers of Christ'. He went further and, stressing wider overtones, called the psalms 'the prayers of Christ and of his church'. As the Jewish people were gathered around their king, so Bonhoeffer says in the psalms the Christian church is gathered around the Messiah who has now come. We could, if we wish, extend this line of re-interpretation. When, for example, we sing the psalms about the Hebrews' deliverance from the slavery of Egypt, we could be praising God for our present deliverance – if we will respond – from the power of evil. For we know we can be set free by the power and love of God brought to us in the life, cross and resurrection of Jesus. In this way the psalms acquire overtones through our experience of Christ and through that of the whole Christian church from the apostles until today.

I love the psalms, but don't mistake me for a starry-eyed enthusiast. Those of us who say psalms frequently know there is always the danger of a dreary, unthinking monotony. The Desert Fathers recognized this and Cassian tells us that they thought it 'better for ten verses to be sung with understanding than for a whole psalm to be poured forth with a bewildered mind'. Yet the very repetition of the psalms can be one of their blessings. Perhaps you have sometimes lived, as I have, overlooking the sea or facing a range of moutains; and isn't one of its charms that it is both always the same and yet always different – if we have learned how to look? Cardinal Basil Hume was talking about how to look at the psalms when he said to his monks at Ampleforth, 'Work hard to *acquire* a love of the psalms.

22

Dear brothers, persevere, persevere.'[3]

Learning to love the psalms as 'the prayers of Christ and of his church' helps us to overcome the desolating loneliness that may accompany our feeling of being the one-man-out-of-step in our largely non-Christian society. When I turn to the psalms in my evening prayers, I often think of how as students preparing for the priesthood we used to sing these same psalms in a gem of a village church looking across the green countryside to the Chiltern hills. We remember one another, we still write and, scattered across the world, we pray the psalms together. And I find the encouragement and strength I often need in our continuing fellowship with Christ and with one another in him through the psalms.

More strikingly Dag Hammarskjöld, the secretary-general of the United Nations, found great strength through the psalms. In *Markings*, his spiritual diary, he quotes them twenty-four times, far more often than any other book of the Bible. He jotted down two verses of trust from the psalms during the Suez crisis, about which incidentally he wrote, 'I don't think I have slept more than two or three hours this past week, but I am doing fine';[4] and then three other verses of confidence in God just before his fatal last journey as he was trying to bring peace to the Congo.

The psalms are the road through life with all its toughness and storms. Not only beneath their praises and rejoicings, but also beneath their complaints and questioning we can sense this confidence that God is, and that he is ever our helper and strength.

'To sing the songs of Israel,' the American scholar, Harvey Guthrie, affirms, 'is to discover a heritage of assurance.'[5]

3

Jesus and *Abba*

Jesus prayed in a way that was startlingly new. So one of his followers asked him, 'Lord, teach us how to pray.' These were men who had prayed all their lives. They had from their mothers' breasts breathed the atmosphere of prayer. They had grown up in a society which believed intensely in God. How fervently they had sung the psalms. They had become men of faith and prayer or they would never have thrown up everything to tramp the roads with Jesus. Some of them had earlier been intimate followers of John the baptizer, the ascetic leader of the day.

It was these men who sensed something unprecedented in Jesus' praying. And the heart of it was hidden in one word from his mother-tongue, *Abba*. When his sayings were translated from this Aramaic into Greek, the *lingua franca* of the Mediterranean, the first Christians sometimes left this word untranslated – and, as we shall see, with good reason.

In brief, *Abba* expresses confidence, a confidence growing out of love, our response to God's unchangeable love. This love-rooted confidence we see in Jesus' way of living as well as in his praying. All this he wants to share with us in our life's journey, come what may.

So if the Desert Fathers have shown us how to start out and the psalmists how to carry on, Jesus gives us in this word *Abba* our magnetic compass to help us keep our sense of direction across all the hills and valleys of this long journey of prayer.

We shall notice too how our guides use this compass. Perhaps Thomas Merton was thinking about this when he wrote, 'The simplicity of the gospels if kept in mind makes false mysticism impossible. Christ has delivered us for ever from the esoteric and the strange.'

We can't have everything clear. There will be mysteries beyond words as we try to follow Jesus' teaching. But first of all we need to ask, 'Have we in our earliest gospels a reliable record of what he said?' Obviously I can only touch on this question. But we must face it intellectually because, as Jesus himself said, we are to love God with our entire personalities, that is, with our minds as well as with our affections. Our prayer cannot be authentic and grow deeper, unless we are with integrity seeking for truth.

We can seek for ourselves, because between the covers of the New Testament we have almost every bit of hard evidence there is about Jesus' teaching. We can – or at least we can be trained to – evaluate this evidence and interpret it. Luke opens his gospel by saying that he has collected information handed down from eye witnesses. We can trace older material behind the gospels. The authors of the earliest gospels give the impression of trying to produce reliable records. They have in general succeeded, according to most scholars, even if not in every detail. I myself have had to study and lecture on the New Testament, and the evidence seems to me quite reliable enough for our purpose.

Dr C. H. Dodd, an outstanding scholar and the director of the translation of the New English Bible, has written:

> When all allowance has been made for these limiting factors – the chances of oral transmission, the effect of translation, the interests of teachers in making the 'sayings' 'contemporary' and simple human fallibilities – it remains that the first three gospels offer a body of sayings on the whole so consistent, so coherent, and withal so distinctive in manner, style and content, that no reasonable critic could doubt, whatever reservations he may have about individual sayings, that we find reflected here the thought of a single, unique teacher.[1]

Of course some of Jesus' sayings may have been altered in details to relate them to the needs of the Greek-speaking churches. But in these modifications no one would have dreamt of adding Aramaic words; so we can be confident that this word *Abba* goes back to the lips of Jesus himself.

In order to be on the safe side, we will concentrate on this word and two well-authenticated, supplementary passages as a basis for Jesus' fundamental teaching on prayer.

Professor Joachim Jeremias, who spent his early life in Palestine, has examined the prayers of Judaism with minute care. These prayers normally address God with elaborate titles, and never as *Abba*. In family life *Abba* was the child's first word for his father, 'Daddy', but it was used too by grown-up sons and daughters as 'dear Father'. So Professor Jeremias says of Jesus' use of *Abba* in his prayer:

> It was something new, something unique and unheard of, that Jesus dared to take this step and to speak with God as a child speaks with his father simply, intimately, securely.[2]

In Gethsemane Jesus prayed *Abba* as a man in his maturity. His loving confidence in God was there being refined like gold in a furnace. 'Abba, Father, all things are possible to thee; take this cup away from me. Yet not what I will, but what thou wilt' (Mark 14.36). Jesus' struggle to pray *Abba* strengthened him to confront with confidence his suffering and death. Discerningly Dr Dodd has written:

> Here is to be found the driving force and source of energy for an almost impossible mission, here certainly the source of the inflexible resolution with which he went, knowingly, to death in the service of his mission.[3]

There is something even more striking. Jesus intends that you and I should actually participate in his own love-rooted confidence in God – both in our praying and in our living.

In the first of these supplementary passages, which is a saying older than our gospels, for it is quoted word for word by both Matthew and Luke, Jesus tells us, 'No one knows the Son except the Father; and no one knows the Father except the Son, and those to whom the Son may choose to reveal him' (Matt. 11.27; Luke 10.23). 'To know' here means, as often in the Bible, not just to recognize, but to know intimately through love. That the Father and the Son should know one another mutually through love is what we should expect Jesus to say. But what is extraordinary is that Jesus says that some men and women can come to know the Father, as the Son does, that is, with a confidence and love like his – indeed which are his.

These people are described as those whom 'the Son chooses'. This does not involve any favouritism, still less any simple predestination. It is only the biblical way of saying – for the Bible seldom speaks of secondary causes – those who themselves choose to respond to the Son's invitation to all. And who these people are is clear from the immediately preceding words, where Jesus says that these things

26

are hidden from 'learned and wise' and revealed to the 'simple'. Those who can know the Father with Jesus' own love-rooted confidence are not those who think they know all the answers, but those who have the openness and loving confidence of children who can truly say *Abba*. These people, Professor Jeremias says, Jesus allows 'to participate in his own communion with God'.[4] Paul, as we shall see, shows how this participation is made possible only through the Spirit.

Our second supplementary passage on prayer chooses itself, the Lord's prayer. Everyone knows that it comes in two forms in the gospels, though clearly it is substantially the same prayer. All modern translations give a longer form in Matthew (6.9–13) and a shorter one in Luke (11.2–4). The latter form begins, 'Father, thy name be hallowed; thy kingdom come.' So when said in Aramaic, it might open with *Abba*. The prayer is not so clear as it looks. I am afraid I haven't room to discuss the various ways it has been understood. You might find it quite useful to write down what this prayer says to you. Here briefly is what strikes me.

The pivot of the prayer, as of all Jesus' teaching in the first three gospels, is, as I see it, 'thy kingdom come'. As Cassian taught, the coming of God's rule is the primary aim of all our praying, rather than our individual relationship with God.

What precedes this pivot clause is our looking towards the Father and adoring him. This is an indispensable preparation. For unless we fix our attention first on God, we shall probably be praying and working not for his kingdom, but for our own. Some kind of contemplation of God himself should go before our interlocked prayer and action.

The petitions, which follow the pivot clause, grow out of it. 'Give us bread' was prayed in a land which knew drought, famine and sieges. And in our concern for his kingdom today we spread out before God as we see them the basic, including the material, needs of our world. Our being ready to be used to meet these needs is an integral element of our prayer.

Equally we and all men need forgiveness. 'Forgive us our sins', or else we cannot be with open eyes concerned with God's rule. 'For we too forgive'; this is not trying to bargain with God. He does not forgive us just as a recompense for our forgiving others. Rather, because God is love, he is every moment trying to pour his forgiveness into our lives. Yet we barricade ourselves behind a hard shell of self-sufficiency. It is this which prevents God's love and forgiveness penetrating into us. But whenever we are ready to own up to

27

our faults and to forgive others, we break this shell and God's grace can flood our hearts. Without forgiving there is no real praying.

Also in our concern for the kingdom, we ask that we may not lose our confidence and initiative, nor be daunted by the evil which may test us, severe as that testing may be.

Profound as the Lord's prayer is, how often we pray it superficially. 'You can't sing a love-song,' it is said, 'unless you are in love.' Pop-singers, who sing for money, don't sound as if they are really in love. Perhaps we can only sing the Lord's song, or pray genuinely the Lord's prayer, when we are loving him or at least desiring to love him. And this, as in human friendship, means that we must make time to be leisurely with the One we want to love more. The *Our Father* might be one of the ways to help us to do this. It is prefaced in Matthew's gospel not by 'pray these words' but 'pray in this way'. This suggests that we might use the *Our Father* not only as a prayer to recite, but rather as a sequence of themes for our own personal prayers. A modern guide in prayer, John Dalrymple, has recommended that we are first still, next remember how close we are to *Abba*, our dear Father, and then for a quarter of an hour slowly and genuinely speak with him in our own words but according to the sequence of the themes of the Lord's prayer.

But we shall never pray well this or any other prayer, unless we are growing towards authenticity – unless, that is, we 'live more nearly as we pray'. We must not be discouraged by so exacting a demand. God does not expect us to get there at once. Real prayer, like real love, takes many years to grow. But both are infinitely worth while working for. In love we only get nearer to it through the loving support of our friend or partner. We can't do it ourselves. Nor can we in prayer. God guarantees to help us through the Spirit of Jesus.

Another wise and encouraging guide of our times, René Voillaume, wrote in the garden of Gethsemane these lines:

Jesus was – and indeed will always remain – the supreme master of prayer; not only because he knew more, but because he prayed better than any man who had ever prayed before him or since. In other words, Jesus *lived* perfect prayer – and that in the midst of a life that was particularly harassing, sometimes almost overpower- ing. The ultimate reason why Jesus must be the master of your prayer, however, is because he alone can put into your minds, your memories, your hearts, the true spirit of prayer, that gratuitous gift of love. No one ever knows how to pray until Jesus himself has taught him – and taught him from within.[5]

4

Paul and the Spirit

Paul had his blind spots. But what a man he was! The Christian church was revolutionized mainly through him. He transformed it from a narrow sect into a dynamic church, spread round the eastern and northern shores of the Mediterranean. It was his love that did it – his intrepid journeys, his unflagging energy, his endless care for others. In his letters we see his affections, his outspokenness and his tears. I remember the book that opened my eyes to those letters, when I was fourteen, as vividly as if I had read it yesterday. Ever since, even in my agnostic days, I have always admired Paul.

He was born in Tarsus, a crowded port, fascinating for a boy, and a stimulating university city, set against the background of the Taurus mountains of Syria. His parents were strict Jews. So he grew up with one foot in a Greek-speaking culture and the other in Judaism. Little did he realize what a preparation this was for his life-work. He was sent to Jerusalem to finish his education. He became fanatical in his hatred of the Christians there. On his way to arrest some of them at Damascus, as everyone knows, he himself experienced a complete *volte-face*, his encounter with the risen Jesus. It was even a physical shock; for a few days he was blind. So momentous was it that he could write in one of his letters that it was for him like the creation story all over again: 'God, who said, "Out of darkness let light shine," has shone in our hearts to give us the light of the knowledge of the glory of God in the face of Jesus Christ' (II Cor. 4.6). So, on the same day, Paul became both believer and apostle: he received together the light that is Christ and his responsibility to share that light with others. We too may have our moments of illumination, perhaps less striking, during worship or in a retreat or while reading a book. Paul's experience may help us to understand and make use of these moments.

Apostle, theologian, founding-father of Christian communities,

Paul was above all a lover, a lover of God, of Jesus the disclosure of God, and his fellowmen and women. 'To me to live is Christ,' he told his friends at Philippi (Phil. 1.21), as a man might say of a beloved wife. 'She's everything to me.' And this was the source of his energy. 'The love of Christ', he wrote, 'impels me' (II Cor. 5.14).

Paul became a man of love through being a man of prayer. His letters teem with praises and meditations, thanksgivings and intercessions. 'Be always joyful; pray continually; give thanks whatever happens; for this is what God in Christ wills for you' (I Thess. 5.16–18). Prayer was not an 'extra' in his life; it was almost like the beating of his heart.

What strikes me about his prayer is first that he had that love-rooted confidence which Jesus had; and secondly that he was convinced that only the Spirit himself can enable us to pray in this way. 'God has sent into our hearts the Spirit of his Son, through whom we cry, "*Abba*, Father"' (Gal. 4.6). Paul would have agreed with the saying of Dr Heiler, 'Prayer is not man's work or discovery or achievement, but God's work in man.'[1]

Some of his prayers we find in his letters. At the beginning of the epistle to the Philippians we can almost overhear him praying. His prayer has a kind of fourfold sequence. We could, if we wish, use this as another kind of prayer-pattern as I suggested in the last chapter we might sometimes use the Lord's prayer.

'I thank my God,' Paul begins, 'whenever I think of you.' It seems, from other letters, that this is normally how he begins his prayers. Even with the cantankerous people at Corinth he starts by thanking God for the signs of his goodness among them. If by contrast we pray ever in a patronizing manner – 'Let us pray for poor old So-and-so, he's got himself into trouble again' – this is the ruination of our prayer.

'My prayers', Paul continues, 'are always joyful.' Joy in prayer comes from our gratitude to God, who is at work in our friends in their co-operation and sometimes in their cussedness. Never is there wheat without tares. And joy is in prayer also because there is always a sparkle of joy in speaking to One we love even when the news is bad.

Then Paul goes on with confidence – 'certain that the One who started the good work in you will bring it to completion'. Many of us on the other hand pray probably more by mere routine rather than with real confidence; often we hardly expect to see anything happen in us or around us through our praying. And Paul's confidence is based not on man's abilities, but on the power of God.

Finally it is in love that Paul prays. 'I hold you in my heart' – not necessarily in warm feelings, because humanly that is not always possible, but in really caring and trying to understand. This is possible because, as he declares, 'I long for you in the heart of Jesus Christ.' He prays in love and he prays for love: 'that your love may grow ever richer'. This love is not blind; rather it will bring 'insight of every kind' and 'true discrimination'. We in our day should pray for right social and economic provisions: but our words are hardly worth the paper they may be printed on – without the dynamic of loving action to carry them through.

The epistles of Paul have been called the gospel of the Spirit. They are full of the Spirit. We are called to 'live in the Spirit', to 'walk in the Spirit', to 'rejoice in the Spirit', to 'sing in the Spirit' and to 'pray in the Spirit'. Through the Spirit we are really able to pray *Abba* with the confidence that filled the heart of Jesus. We are not then to live weak, anxious lives, but to pray and live as sons confident in our Father's love, just because the Spirit himself 'makes us sons' enabling us to cry, *Abba*, Father' (Rom. 8.15). We may sometimes feel weak and incapable of real prayer, and all that we can then manage are inarticulate desires. But Paul encourages us by telling us that in these inarticulate aspirations the Spirit is truly praying within us and God understands. Not only does God understand; but in whatever happens he is also co-operating with us for our true good.

> The Spirit comes to the aid of our weakness. We do not even know how we ought to pray, but through our inarticulate groans the Spirit himself is pleading for us, and God who searches our inmost being knows what the Spirit means, because he pleads for God's own people in God's own way; and in everything, as we know, he co-operates for good with those who love God (Rom. 8.26–28 NEB).

Our ordinary prayers as Christians, alone or with others, should then be prayers of confidence, '*Abba*, Father,' through the Holy Spirit who himself enables us to pray in this way. In words or in silence let us ask his help. So I often begin, 'Holy Spirit, help me to pray, because by myself I can't really pray.' But let us watch that this asking doesn't itself become mere routine.

At times Paul had abnormal experiences in prayer, 'visions and revelations granted by the Lord', as he called them (II Cor. 12.1), though he was reluctant to speak of them (II Cor. 12.1–4). We shall see something similar in Mother Julian of Norwich and in Teresa of Avila. We should not – and Teresa's guide, John of the Cross, would agree with this – be over-impressed by these experiences, but regard them as physical symptoms which sometimes accompany spiritual gifts, rather like Paul's temporary blindness after his conversion.

Another form of prayer in New Testament times was ecstatic 'speaking with tongues'. This has reappeared in the recent charismatic movement. I write as a friend of that movement, because I have seen in many countries how it can deepen prayer and love. No one would say that 'speaking with tongues' is the chief sign of the movement. The evidence of the New Testament shows, I think, that this sign was less widespread than is sometimes supposed. Where 'speaking with tongues' is overvalued, it can become divisive, as it was at Corinth. But Paul did not forbid it; in fact he himself was gifted in this way (I Cor. 14.18). But he said that more valuable for the Christian community is prophecy, which is, I presume, speaking clearly of the practical implications of our fellowship with God through Christ. Paul also never undervalued our intellect; 'I would rather speak five intelligible words,' he wrote, 'for the benefit of others as well as myself, than thousands of words in the language of ecstasy' (I Cor. 14.19).

In his enumeration of the gifts of the Spirit in the Christian community Paul first put apostles, next prophets, then teachers and at the end of the list the gift of tongues. Clearly not all are called to be apostles or prophets or teachers; neither, so he implied, are all expected to speak with tongues. He said, 'Put love first' (I Cor. 14.1); and so would members of the charismatic movement. We are all agreed that all gifts are to be tested by whether they increase love or not. 'I may speak in tongues of men or of angels, but if I am without love, I am a sounding gong and a clanging cymbal' (I Cor. 13.1).

What matters most is perseverance in love and in prayer through the power of the Spirit. Engrossed as Paul was in his journeys, his correspondence, his day-to-day ministry to individuals and to these young Christian communities, yet always he could say, 'All I care for is to know Christ, to experience the power of his resurrection, and to share his sufferings' (Phil. 3.10).

Paul's first concern was – through praying and loving – to come more and more to know Jesus. Then he found out that through knowing Christ he experienced in himself the power of Christ's resurrection. He was able to carry his immense load of work not in his own strength alone, but in that power of God which raised Jesus from the dead. Next, he discovered that he received this power of Christ's resurrection only in proportion that he was sharing in Christ's sufferings. So in the hardships and pressures of life, Paul knew that he was not alone, but with Jesus in *his* sufferings. 'In my flesh,' Paul could write, 'I complete what is lacking in Christ's afflictions' (Col. 1.24).

This is what we also are called to in a life of true prayer. It will always be beyond our achievement. But we don't let ourselves give in to discouragement or cease to try. 'I do not reckon to have got hold of it yet,' Paul himself went on to say. 'All I can say is this: forgetting what is behind me and reaching out for what lies ahead, I press on' (Phil. 3.13).

C'est l'oeuvre d'une vie à recommencer chaque matin.[2] 'To love and to pray with confidence', so wrote René Voillaume, 'is the task of a lifetime. It needs to be begun afresh every day.' In the power of the Spirit, Paul affirms, we can tackle this confidently: 'Give yourselves wholly to prayer and entreaty; pray on every occasion in the power of the Spirit' (Eph. 5.18–20).

5

John and God's Love

John's gospel is 'a pool in which a child may wade and an elephant may swim'.[1] So Dr Leon Morris opens his 900-page commentary on it. It is easy to see how unsophisticated and sophisticated are gripped by John. Augustine understood why; 'Show me a lover,' he wrote, 'and he will understand this gospel.' I have quite lost count of all the books I have read on John, and I can now only share with you the conviction they have left on me: this gospel is the fruit of a lifetime's meditation.

The fundamental and particular truth which John makes clear to us for our present search for the heart of prayer is that prayer is our response to God's love. John in his first letter affirms, 'We love, because God first of all loved us.'

But does God really love us? This is the problem for many people. There are times when there seems to be no sign of God, still less of his love. Life is like the sky covered with black clouds of tragedy and injustice in the world – and perhaps depression and frustration in our own lives. We cannot explain away the reality of these evils. But – and this is the basic disclosure in John and in the New Testament – always piercing those ominous clouds there *is* a beam of sunlight which makes us sure that beyond the blackness there is light and love.

That beam is Jesus, and the truth about him is crystallized out for us in John's words about Jesus – 'He who has seen me has seen the Father.' He who has seen the love that is in Jesus has seen God's love. That love we are assured – in spite of all these evils – is at the heart of everything. And this divine love, as we can tell from the gospels, is not a vague, generalized benevolence; it is a love personally focused, just like the love of Jesus focused, for example, on Nicodemus in his doubts, on the woman at the well of Samaria in her evasiveness and on Mary and John in the darkness of Good Friday.

Incidentally, this is how I would understand 'God's providence' mentioned in the psalms. I have to write briefly, but for me providence is not so much that God directly sends good fortune or misfortune, but rather that God with his love is present in every situation. Therefore, as Paul said, 'In everything God co-operates for good with those who love him' (Rom. 8.28).

But how can we be steadily and deeply convinced that God with his unchangeable love is present at every moment and in every situation? We need clear thinking. It is no good trying to dodge intellectual difficulties. But we all know that intellect alone – important as it is – cannot give us all the staying power we need. This, as we shall soon see, is just where meditation helps.

John has painted a portrait of our Lord, while the earlier gospel-writers had, roughly speaking, sketched the events of his life. Dr Bultmann contrasts the 'medley of items in the early gospels and fundamentally a single theme, the person of Jesus, in John's gospel'.[3] So in this last gospel we can as in a master-portrait see through the outward actions to the inner character of Jesus, to his hidden communion with the Father, which flooded his life with love.

John had a great deal of material about Jesus, but he selected certain actions and words with a particular aim, and he tells us why: 'that believing you may have life in his name' (John 20.31). He wants all his readers to have 'life', by a growing confidence in God through Jesus. 'Life' or 'eternal life', as John often calls it, means that real fellowship with God, which we can already have now, and which will come to its full richness in eternity. John invites us to grow into this essential confidence in God by meditating on these works and words of Jesus.

John keeps this aim before him as, chapter by chapter, he paints this gospel portrait. The first eighteen verses, a preface, stand by themselves. His fundamental theme, 'He who has seen me has seen the Father', is announced in terms more theological: 'The Word became flesh; he came to dwell among us'; that is, God's own disclosure of himself, the love that is himself, became man and in the man Jesus he actually lived among us. How stupendous a happening this was, John goes on to express in personal terms. 'No one has ever seen God; but God's only Son, he who is nearest to the Father's heart, he has made him known' (John 1.14–18).

Then the plan of this gospel falls into two parts. The first part (up to the end of chapter 12) I would like to call 'Signs, Dialogues and

Commitment'. It contains miracles, told at some length, with dialogues and discourses growing out of them. The earlier gospel-writers recounted many more 'miracles', 'wonder-works', and they told them chiefly, though not entirely, as expressions of Jesus' human compassion for people. On the other hand, John calls them 'signs', and he uses them as windows to let the divine love of the Father shine with power into the darkness of this world. Then those who take part in John's dialogues or listen to his discourses are invited to put their confidence increasingly in Jesus, the Messiah, the Son of God, and to commit themselves to him. Here is one example. In chapter 6 we have the 'sign' of the feeding of the five thousand; this merges into a dialogue about the bread of life; then the crowds fade away, and the narrative culminates in Peter's commitment to following Christ in the words: 'We have come to believe and to recognize that you are the Holy One of God.'

The second part of the gospel (chapters 13–20), where the word 'love' is used four times more often than in the first part, I would entitle 'Love and Glory'. Its first section, Love, is about the night in the upper room before the Lord's death (chapters 13–17); and its second section, Glory, is about his passion and resurrection (chapters 18–20).

In its first section, Love, if I may slightly simplify, we have in chapter 13 the expression of the Lord's love in washing the disciples' feet, and its significance for us. In the following chapter we see, in spite of the anxieties of that night, – and of our world today – the unchangeable love of God disclosed for us in Jesus: 'He who has seen me has seen the Father.'

The fifteenth chapter links God's love in Jesus to our life in the world. 'I am the vine, and you the branches. He who dwells in me, as I dwell in him, bears much fruit; for apart from me you can do nothing.' And it is through love that we abide in Jesus; for he says, 'Dwell in my love,' in the same way that he dwells in the Father's love. Then as a consequence we are called to love one another with the love with which he loves us. In this love we are interlocked with one another as the branches are, because we are all part of the true vine, who is Christ. The next chapter is largely about the Spirit, that is, God at work within us; we shall see that this chapter helps us to see how John composed his gospel. The seventeenth chapter is a prayer, first of all for the disciples. Then it widens to embrace those who will in the future commit themselves to God. It asks that believers may be knit together so manifestly by love that the world itself, through seeing this love, may finally be drawn to God. This cannot happen by human efforts alone, however sincere. Though it requires our co-operation, it is fundamentally a gift from above, for the Lord is portrayed asking 'that the love thou, Father, hast for me may be in them'.

In its second section, Glory (chapters 18–20), the passion and resurrection are for John one thing; they are complementary facets of the glory of love, love revealed and then love triumphant. It was a little earlier, in fact when Judas the betrayer was leaving the upper room, that the words were said, 'Now the Son of man is glorified' (John 13.31), because at that moment Judas was setting in motion the events that would lead up to the crucifixion. In John's eyes the passion is already the glory, because it is the culminating point of Jesus' unswerving love, that is, of God's eternal love. And this is why Jesus declares, as he completes on the cross his offering of a lifetime of love, 'It is finished' – it is accomplished (John 19.30). For this was not a sigh of relief at the end of his pain, but an utterance of triumph that his task of love was now carried through. 'I have glorified thee on earth by completing the work which thou gavest me to do' (John 17.4).

'Calvary,' Bishop Michael Ramsey has written about John's gospel, 'is no disaster which needs the resurrection to reverse it, but a victory so signal that the resurrection follows quickly to seal it. John thinks of the glorifying of Jesus as completed on Easter day. As soon as the glorifying is accomplished, the Spirit can then be given.' [3] To John the 'ascension', that is, the 'glorifying of Jesus', and also the coming of the Spirit, are parts of the same mystery of the Lord's death and resurrection. For in John's gospel it is on Easter morning that Jesus says to Mary Magdalen, 'I am ascending to my Father and your Father'; and it is on Easter evening that Jesus says to his disciples, 'Receive the Holy Spirit' and at once gives them the Spirit.

On the following Sunday this gospel closes (for chapter 21 is a later addition to it) with Thomas' commitment to Jesus in confidence: 'My Lord and my God' and then the Lord's blessing on all those who in the future are to be drawn to the same commitment: 'Blessed are those who have not seen – and yet have believed.'

We turn now to the composition of this remarkable gospel. How do you think it was written? I have come to the conclusion that John felt inspired to weave together two precious things – the story of the Jesus who walked in Galilee and Jerusalem, and the experience of the same Jesus, now risen and glorified, whom John – and generations of Christians – have truly met in prayer and sacrament, in love of our neighbours and in meditation. Perhaps we sense this weaving together most deeply in the words and prayers of the upper room: 'Although Jesus speaks at the Last Supper,' declares Professor Raymond Brown of the Roman Pontifical Biblical Commission; 'yet he is really speaking from heaven.'[4] This was put most penetratingly by Browning in his poem, *A Death in the Desert*:

> To me, that story – ay, that life and death
> Of which I wrote 'it was' – to me, it is.

It was through the Spirit that John had long meditated on the actions and words of Jesus; and now he felt inspired by the Spirit to compose his gospel. Indeed for him both the meditating and the writing were part at least of the fulfilment of words from his gospel: 'The Holy Spirit, whom the Father will send in my name, will teach you everything, and will call to mind all that I have told you' (John 14.26); and 'He will guide you into all truth. He will glorify me, for everything that he makes known to you he will draw from what is mine' (John 16.13–14).

To receive all that John was inspired to offer us, we need intellectual study; but we need meditation too. If this gospel was composed meditatively, we should receive it meditatively.

In the present-day search for a deeper relationship with God, there is a growing interest in meditation. There are so many ways of meditating that we need to find out, probably with the help of a guide, what kind of meditation would most help us, where we are now. I hesitate to try to give you advice here, because those who may well read this book will be of such different temperaments and at such different stages on the journey of prayer. But some of you may be wishing to make a start and need some advice not too vague. So may I say roughly what I try to do? I will try to illustrate it with a passage from John. I am not an expert, and I vary my method from time to time. You may find some other way more effective for you.

I have frequently to remind myself of my aim in meditation. If people don't do this, they often get tired of meditation and either give it up or else make it a mere formal habit. Bible study is not meditation, although it may lead to it. In Bible study we look for something new. But in meditation our aim is primarily to be drawn nearer to God in love. We are made for this. We need it as we need friendship. Meditation is as natural to us as making friends.

When a letter comes from a close friend, you hold it in your hand. You don't have to imagine it; it is actually sent, given to you. It is the same with the scriptures in meditation. You read your friend's letter first for the news it contains. You may next feel close to your friend and perhaps conscious of his affection. Then you may pick out and treasure certain words or turns of phrase, which may stay with you during the day, however busy you are. My kind of meditation is something like this.

I personally find it best to arrange my time for meditative prayer early in the day before the telephone begins to ring. But I like first to read over the passage the evening before. Let us suppose I am going through John. I notice the setting of the passage in the general plan of the gospel. Then I read over a paragraph, perhaps a dozen verses. I myself normally use the biblical text by itself, but perhaps that is because I have over the years done a good deal of reading about it. If I come across a passage which is beyond me, I leave it out, though I try later on to find someone who could explain it to me.

To make things clear, let me say what I would probably do with those verses about Christ the vine and ourselves its branches in John 15.5-11. On the previous evening after reading them through, I would look for phrases likely to open doors of prayer for me. These might be 'You can bear no fruit, unless you depend on me'; 'dwell in my love' and 'that my joy might be in you and your joy complete'. I would let these verses simmer in my mind.

The next morning I can start at once: no leafing through the bible to find a suitable passage. I normally like to sit on a firm, upright chair, alert but relaxed. Reading a friend's letter can be a real meeting. So in meditation I first settle down and, as it were, 'tune myself in'. But don't misunderstand me. None of us can always 'feel' God's presence, yet we can always remember it. And breathing deeply and slowly helps me to quieten down. With the breathing I ask for the help of the Holy Spirit, remembering, as Paul said, that only through the Holy Spirit can we truly pray *Abba*.

Then often just one phrase is enough for me, though I sometimes need more. I ponder over the phrases from my passage. I turn my reflections at once into words of prayer to God. Meditation is not speculation, but rather it is opening ourselves to God's love, and responding with our confidence and love. Often we do not need

39

many words. As we make time to meditate regularly like this, a relationship of real love between God and ourselves is gradually built up; and like human friendship and love, it brings us strength and joy.

This kind of meditative praying needs to be kept rooted in everyday living. So it is useful to plan to do some little thing in the coming day to give concrete expression to this love, even if it is only to reply to a letter or to ring up a lonely person. Human friendship and love often starts to grow quickly or slowly in unexpected ways; but then we have to build it up together by frequent words of appreciation and by countless practical acts of kindness.

We should try not to hurry away from our times of prayer. With our friends we often find it hard to tear ourselves away. And afterwards something they have said goes on echoing in our hearts, as phrases from their letters do. So a phrase from our meditation could go on ringing inside us even in our busy days, as Cassian said, reminding us of the one who loves us and whom we wish to love in return more and more. So I can well understand how William Temple could write, 'For as long as I can remember I have had more love for St John's gospel than for any other book.'[5]

6

Mother Julian and *The Cloud of Unknowing*

When I was staying with an English friend in Malaysia, he told me that what he there missed most of all was our round of the seasons and especially the coming of spring with the increasing song of birds and fresh green leaves unfolding. And when we trace the course of prayer down the centuries, we are enchanted with a similar recurring wonder of the springtime of the Spirit.

We started our journey with the Desert Fathers and John Cassian in their springtime. That led us to the psalmists, because they so valued the psalms for their prayer. The psalms in turn brought us to the New Testament, the springtime of prayer *par excellence* – to Jesus, Paul and John. We have, I think, by now picked up the basic principles for our journey into prayer. As we go on, we will watch these principles really coming to life in our fellowmen and women from the Middle Ages until today.

The fourteenth century in medieval England was another springtime – one shared with countries across the North Sea. There was a widespread love of Jesus, human and divine, and much pondering on the scenes of his passion through which God's love shines like sunlight. This devotion inspired the magnificent Gothic cathedrals, their incomparable stained glass, their illuminated manuscripts, mystery plays and pilgrimages. Their scholars too shared a fellowship without frontiers.

Books began to be written in the English of Langland's *Piers Plowman* and Chaucer's *Canterbury Tales* rather than in Latin or Norman-French. Within this springtime of the vernacular, our English writers on prayer, each strongly individual, made a leap forward like the opening of early flowers. We can group their books roughly into books of experience and books of instruction. Mother Julian's *Revelations of Divine Love* belongs to the first, and the anonymous *Cloud of Unknowing* to the second.

I must admit that when I first turned to Mother Julian's book I did so with some hesitation. I feared that she might be a strange deluded person. I can now see how wrong I was. Her experiences in prayer produced such genuine, caring love that no discerning guide would doubt their authenticity. The depths of her experience can still speak to our hearts and minds.

Julian was born in 1342 in the prosperous city of Norwich, with its soaring cathedral spire, its castle and sixty churches. You can still see her cell, the size of a small living-room, two steps down from the medieval church of St Peter and St Julian – another Julian. The cell has two windows, one opening into the church, through which she could receive communion; the other looking into a garden, and here people came to ask for spiritual guidance. She lived for many years as an anchoress, reading, writing, meditating, interceding – nothing unusual in those days. She received her 'shewings' at home, I think, and then, after the usual careful testing, became an anchoress.

Mother Julian tells us that when she was thirty she had a severe illness and all thought she was dying. Then the pain ceased and between four and nine o'clock in the morning of 8 May 1373 she received fifteen 'shewings'. She pretended to the priest by her bedside that she had been delirious, that these 'happenings' were unreal; then quickly and deeply repented of this deceit. She fell asleep. She dreamt she was attacked by the devil – an 'ugly shewing unlike any of the others'. She had her last, her sixteenth, 'shewing' of Jesus, divine and human, sitting enthroned in her heart; 'for in us,' she says, 'is he completely at home'. Then she was told to treasure and ponder over all she had received. 'Take it, believe it, hold on to it, comfort yourself with it and trust it.'

Mother Julian wrote her book in its longer form – two versions exists – only after twenty years of meditating on these experiences. She explained that these 'shewings' came to her in three ways: 'by physical sight, by words formed in my intellect, and by spiritual sight'; and of the last she says, 'I may never fully tell it'. These 'shewings' are, as it were, the 'take-off' for her profound meditations.

What most impresses me in these meditations is Julian's deep, unshakeable assurance that we are each personally loved by God. She says, like John, that it is God's loving us which is basic, not our loving him. The practical importance of this is clear. It could bring us an inner serenity. It could also help us to build up caring friendships with many people, when we can look at them in the light of God's love for them.

Mother Julian puts this truth in her own vivid way. God – as Father, as Son, as Holy Spirit – is ceaselessly reaching out to us in love. God loves us so compassionately that Julian speaks of the Father and of the Son as 'our mother'. 'God is as really our mother as he is our father.' Even more strikingly she writes, 'The human mother will suckle her child with her own milk, but our beloved mother Jesus feeds us with himself, and, with the most tender courtesy, does it by means of the holy sacrament'. Further, as we mature in confidence and in prayer, our Lord treats us 'like a wise mother, who changes her methods, but not her love'.

There is not only tenderness in our Lord's love, but also courageous strength. 'In his love,' she says, 'he has done all his works.' But the strength of his love is disclosed above all in his passion and cross, which are so real to Mother Julian. Everything he did to free us from evil was done in the power of love.

As she meditated on this love, Christ spoke inwardly to her. 'See how I have loved you. My dearest, look at your Lord, your God, your maker and your endless joy.' And she knew she was called to respond to him. 'Because I love you, enjoy me! This will please me most of all.'

Whatever she learned of God's love Julian knew was for everyone, not just for herself. 'For it is God's will that you should receive it with great joy and pleasure, as if Jesus had showed it to you all.' And however much any of us fails, she was confident that 'our falling does not hinder him from loving us'. In the end, she believed, all will be gathered together into one in Christ, for he said, 'Look, I am God. I am in all. I am guiding everything towards the end I ordained for it from the first, by the same might, wisdom and love with which I made it. How can anything be wrong?'

But we may still feel like asking, 'Those words are attractive, but are they true? What about the problem of evil and suffering?' Mother Julian did not close her eyes to the problem. She had been through suffering. In Norwich she saw the Black Death and two other plagues. She heard of the Peasants' Revolt and its suppression. Julian never put down these evils, as many did at that time, to God's anger. 'There is no anger in God,' she said. She meant, as I suppose the New Testament does, that God is never angry as men are, vindictively; rather, that what may be called God's anger is his love inevitably and impersonally removing evil in its path.

But if her words 'God will make everything right' mean that all will be finally saved, Julian knows she is going against the doctrine of her church – yet she intends to be loyal to the church. So she remains perplexed about why God permits evil in his creation. The only answer she received was that all would be well in the end. 'Sin is behovable' (that is, inevitable), 'but all shall be well, and all shall be well, and all manner of things shall be well.'

Her book is a book of experience and of encouragement. 'God said not, "You shall not be tempested, you shall not be afflicted" but "You shall not be overcome".' Her confidence springs from God's disclosure of his love. Mother Julian encourages us to respond, as she did, with love to love: 'Would you know our Lord's meaning in this thing?' she writes. 'Know it well. Love was his meaning. Who showed it you? Love. What did he show you? Love. Why did he show it? For love.' So she sends us on our way – 'Live gladly and gaily because of his love.'

How can we share her love-rooted confidence? Meditation, as we have seen, will help us. *The Cloud of Unknowing* can take us a step further.

This is a book of instruction, but certainly not a dry textbook. It comes warm with experience. No one knows who the author was. He is clearly a scholar, who writes with directness and charm. He has a sense of humour too; he tells us of preachers who wave their arms about as if they were swimming in the ocean. But there is none of this artificiality, he says, in real religion; it rather gives you 'the knack of being at home with everyone'. He stresses reading or hearing the Bible as a real foundation for a life of prayer. He is a modest man, and says, 'I have still a very long way to go myself'. If we cannot understand this book, he thinks we had better give it a second try; then, if we still can't, he says, 'Look for another guide.'

He has helped me a good deal, though he writes for those further on the road of prayer than I am. We should I think follow spiritual guides appreciatively, though never blindly; and on two points I can't agree with him. First, he implies that if you are going deeply into prayer, you had better 'get out of the world' and become an anchoress, nun or monk. This was of course the common opinion of the Middle Ages. Secondly, he seems to me to work, if I may say so, with a one-sided idea of God. Let me try to explain briefly. Christians hold two truths together, that God is both the creator of infinite power, far, far beyond us, yet he is also, paradoxically, in his love intimately close to us. The author of *The Cloud* over-emphasizes the first. He had translated and been influenced by a book which had put this point of view forcibly. The book, originally written by a fifth-century Syrian monk, was erroneously ascribed to Dionysius the Areopagite, an Athenian convert of Paul, and so was regarded as being almost as authoritative as Paul's epistles.

But *The Cloud* can help us most, I think, if we keep in mind that this God, who is infinite, indescribable, has also crossed the gap between himself and us through the life, death and resurrection of Christ, so that we can now speak to him as *Abba* through the power of the Spirit, and as Mother Julian would say 'in true homely manner'.

This book fell into my hands, as often seems to happen, just when I needed it. Pardon my writing so personally. There is a kind of ebb and flow in my prayers. I am no expert. I was continuing to read each night a few verses of the Bible, as I said in the last chapter, so as to have something to start from the next morning. But in my meditations I was becoming more and more distracted, I was not reflecting so much, and I felt less and less inclined to turn my prayers into words. Sometimes I even wondered whether I was wasting my time. I have since learned that this change is quite normal; it may happen to you, or perhaps has done so already.

The Cloud came to me like a godsend. We are, it says, at this stage of our prayer like climbers about half-way up a mountain in the morning. Above us is 'the cloud of unknowing' which hides the summit from our view. But beneath our feet lies quite a different cloud – it is in the bottom of the valley where the warmth of the morning is making the moisture rise; and it is called 'the cloud of forgetting'.

When we try to settle down for our prayer, we are often distracted with all sorts of thoughts – things we have forgotten to do, words said to us which have annoyed us, anxieties about the future. But we must not be discouraged. It happens to almost everyone. There is a proper time, our author says, to analyse these thoughts, but it is not now. It's no good struggling with them. We must learn how to let them slip away down the mountainside and 'to cover them with the thick cloud of forgetting'.

And then we must look up steadily to the peak where, as it were, God enfolds himself in the other luminous cloud, 'the cloud of unknowing'. But when we have arrived at this point in our journey, we often find we cannot look up to God and keep our attention on him, as we used to do, by reflecting on scripture, or by any other way of thinking. That method used to work, but now it often doesn't. Our author says, 'God may well be loved, but not thought' – at this stage at least of the climb: and again, 'By love he can be caught and held, but by thinking never'. Rather he tells us, 'Strike that thick cloud of unknowing with the sharp dart of longing love and on no account whatever think of giving it up'. Prayer still requires sustained effort, but of another kind. 'Short prayer', he adds, 'penetrates heaven.' Nor do we now need to analyse the precise meaning of the words we use. Rather it is more like lovers saying 'I love you' simply to express and deepen their love for each other. That is why our author says, 'The shorter the word the better, being more like the working of the Spirit – a word like "God" or "Love".'

Then we discover the more we focus our attention directly on God in his love, the more likely we are to receive his love and the more we shall want to respond to him. 'It is characteristic of the true lover that the more he loves, the more he wants to love,' so our author reminds us. He writes persuasively, and he could have been, I think, even more persuasive if he had helped us above all to explore the depths of Jesus' word *Abba*.

At the end of my time of praying I unhurriedly remember just a few people, who are close to me or who especially need my prayers, and I ask that we may be fellow-sharers in God's love. Then I say very slowly the Lord's prayer that God's kingdom may come to all men.

And should I feel on some days lazy and disinclined to pray, I think of those I wish to help and I remember that perhaps they may lose something, if I fail to persevere in prayer. And *The Cloud* reminds us that those who are united to God by love are by that same love united to one another.

7

Ignatius Loyola and Teresa of Avila

In the century after Mother Julian many were shocked by corruption and superficiality in the church. Luther in 1517 launched the Reformation by pinning his ninety-five Protestant Theses on the church door at Wittenberg. But already changes had begun within the Catholic church. Cardinal Ximenes, the bishop primate of Spain from 1495 to 1517, carried through a reforming policy and particularly promoted biblical study.

Indeed there was a breakthrough in Spain with a longing for prayer deep and real. Two of its inspirers, both profoundly contemplative, were Teresa of Avila (1515–1582), a warm-hearted woman, and, a little older, Ignatius Loyola (1491–1556), so matter-of-fact at first sight that, as a Jesuit biographer puts it, beside Teresa and John of the Cross Ignatius sounds like 'a sparrow among nightingales';[1] but the moving, though cryptic, journal of his last years in Rome shows how deeply contemplative his prayer was.[2]

Ignatius was the eleventh and unexpected child born in a small Basque castle in a green, wooded valley ten miles from the Bay of Biscay in sight of the Pyrenees. The family was arrogantly Catholic and had an untamed vitality. Ignatius' father and three brothers had illegitimate children. Two brothers were among the earliest to sail to America. The only education Ignatius had was training in arms and at court. At the age of twenty-six, in a foolhardy effort to defend the neighbouring castle of Pamplona against the French, he was wounded by a cannon-ball. He bore stoically, without any anaesthetic, his leg being badly set, broken again, re-set and stretched. Convalescing, he wanted something to read, some romance of knights and their ladies. But the only books available were lives of the saints and a massive *Life of Christ* by Ludolph the Carthusian. In those long hours of reading, solitude and prayer, Jesus for the first time became real to Ignatius. A question pressed itself upon him: should he spend his life in the service of this Lord or not?

He made his choice. Once he was fit he rode 400 miles to the shrine of the Black Madonna in the Benedictine Abbey high up in a weirdly-shaped mountain at Montserrat. Ignatius prayed for three days, he examined his life and was then absolved. He spent the last night in vigil, left his sword in the shrine and stepped out into a new life in the rough clothes of a pilgrim. He was determined to walk in the footsteps of his Lord in the Holy Land. But instead of going to the port of Barcelona, he took the opposite road, which I have followed, for twenty miles to the small town of Manresa. He needed a few days to write in his journal. This record of his decisive choice is the seed of his book, the *Spiritual Exercises*. Those few days grew into the ten most crucial months in his life. Ignatius the aristocrat begged his food in the narrow streets of Manresa and lodged where he could. He worshipped in the Dominicans' basilica with its flying buttresses on the hill, read again and again the Lord's passion, and discovered *The Imitation of Christ* by Thomas à Kempis, 'my dearest book', as he called it. Above all he spent countless solitary hours in thistle-choked caves (one of which is now a chapel), looking across the Cardoner river back to his holy mountain. He experienced the abysses of spiritual life and then the ascent, far steeper than the climb to Montserrat, towards the summit of contemplative praying. One day, at a spot where the Cardoner runs deeply, he received spiritual illumination that gave him more, he tells us, than all the rest of his years of prayer and study put together. There, where he had lived them, this Basque wrote in his bad Spanish much of the *Spiritual Exercises*.

Now he made his pilgrimage to the Holy Land, begging his bread by road and enduring storms by sea. Deeply moved, he spent a month tracing the steps of Jesus and filling his memory with gospel scenes, more material for his *Spiritual Exercises*. He wished to stay longer to preach to the Moslems or just to live among them a life of austerity and prayer, as Charles de Foucauld did in our century. But the Franciscans, who were already guardians of the holy places, refused to let him.

The love which burned in his heart drove him on to preach Jesus fully in western Europe, now hardened into Catholic and Protestant and already beginning to be undermined by scepticism. Ignatius saw that he must himself be educated and also find companions dedicated completely, like himself, to this task. Back in Barcelona, now in

48

his thirties, he sat with schoolboys at their benches, learning Latin grammar.

Eventually study took him for seven years to Paris. Ignatius arrived as Calvin left. His reaction against Protestantism now leaves its mark on his writing. He drew around him six fellow-students whom he guided one by one through the *Spiritual Exercises*. Then early on the feast of the Assumption 1534, in a chapel of the Holy Martyrs on Montmartre – which with difficulty I found in the basement now of a centre for rehabilitation of prisoners – the seven friends vowed themselves to poverty, to chastity and to making a Holy Land pilgrimage or, if this last were not possible, to going to Rome to put themselves entirely at the disposal of the pope. It was the latter choice that they finally fulfilled and so they became the Society of Jesus.

Ignatius completed his *Spiritual Exercises* at Rome in 1546, a book he had lived with for nearly thirty years. It is the distillation of his own profound experiences and of his observations as he guided others. It is a carefully-planned series of meditations, nearly all biblical. Its aim is to help us to pray authentically and then, unswayed by prejudices, to choose deliberately to serve the Lord, as Ignatius did, either in our present situation or in some new vocation. It is a training manual for those who will guide others in retreat. Originally these retreats were given to one person alone and lasted four weeks. I have twice gained much from that experience myself. In many places retreats for a week or for a weekend are now arranged for all sorts of people.[3] But the aim remains unobtrusively the same – and often the general sequence of the meditations. It was in a short retreat that I experienced the greatest turning-point in my life. Grateful for that blessing, I am happy to be asked to conduct retreats in many countries. Unfortunately the *Exercises* have sometimes been allowed to degenerate into a mere meditation drill. But Ignatius himself was always sensitive, flexible and ready to lead people to more simple, contemplative praying; he wrote that some may find one or two words from the Lord's prayer enough for a whole hour of prayer.

At Rome Ignatius had to become an administrator, but he never became cold or remote. With his own hands he took care of the starving in a bitter winter in Rome. He preached in the streets in his curious mixture of Spanish and Italian. When the pope finally authorized his Society, Ignatius walked with his companions at dawn in Easter week to St Paul's outside the city walls, said mass there before a thirteenth-century mosaic of Mary – I well remember it – and embraced his companions, he tells us, 'with tears of joy in his eyes'. It was their dedication at Montmartre all over again – and fulfilled. Then for fifteen years, while his Society was growing to a thousand members, he was more or less tied to his little office. We can still see it with its heavy joists. From his seven last years, 6,641 of his letters survive. He was always known as 'the little Spaniard' – he was only 5′ 3″ – 'with a limp, and laughing eyes'. The shining stars, the flowers in a garden, the sound of a well-loved hymn could transport him in his incessant work 'to the seventh heaven', to which he said the graces of Manresa were only a gentle introduction. And how he was loved! One of his earliest companions, now thousands of miles off in the Far East, could read only with tears the ending of his letters: 'Eternally yours, without my being able to forget you, Ignatius.'

Teresa was born in the city of Avila with its granite walls on the bare Castilian plateau, higher than Vesuvius. The air is as clear as crystal; you can see for miles. The native village of her pupil-partner, the diminutive John of the Cross, was close at hand. Castile seems to have given them both a clarity, a lightness of touch, a relentless though never gloomy asceticism; and to John, a logic as hard as the local rock.

But Teresa did not begin that way. In real prayer she was a late starter. She came from a comfortably-off family, one of twelve children. She was only thirteen when her mother died at the age of thirty-three, probably worn out by childbearing. Secretly Teresa devoured the kind of romances Ignatius had asked for during his convalescence. She was a pleasure-loving girl. Her strict father sent her to a convent 'finishing school'.

She wrote later on that she was afraid of marriage. So at twenty-one she went to the Carmelite convent of the Incarnation, with its 150 nuns, half a mile outside the city walls – rather reluctantly, for she admitted she had no love of God to compensate for her love of her home. She started with what she called 'twenty years on a stormy sea'; and soon had alarming illnesses, probably psychosomatic. She tried to interest herself in prayer, but she always prayed from a book; and one of her books of prayer is still preserved at the convent, with its yellow pages, dog-eared and heavily marked. Sometimes she tells us she just watched the slow hands of the clock when she was supposed to be praying. For a year she gave up even trying to meditate.

Then a change came; and she wrote, 'I could not possibly doubt that the Lord was within me and I in him'. She began to have visions 'with the eyes of the soul' and to hear a voice 'inwardly'. She herself feared that these might be delusions, and two of her advisers were very critical about them. Then she consulted one of the Jesuits. 'I was attracted to them by my knowledge of their method of life and prayer,' she wrote. He encouraged her to press on, and she felt the need of a stricter life than that at the convent of the Incarnation.

Her confessors told her to write her life. She gave it the sub-title 'Of the Mercies of God'. It was written at breakneck speed. It says much about the problems of beginners. As she advances in prayer, Teresa finds herself praying to the Lord in 'that simple way in which I often speak to him without knowing what I am going to say, for it is love that speaks' (*Life*, xxxiv. 1. 235) – the *Abba* prayer indeed.

At last she managed to found – in the teeth of opposition – an austere convent for thirteen sisters at St Joseph's, Avila. There she lived with deepening prayer what she called 'the five most restful years of my life', and wrote *The Way of Perfection*, a manual for her nuns. Next she went on to found her second convent at Medina del Campo, where, old enough to be his mother, she met John of the Cross. She persuaded him to work for the corresponding reform for the Carmelite monks, and he had an even tougher struggle. If Teresa is everyone's writer on prayer, with her charm and spontaneity, he is the theologian's writer on prayer, clear, logical, demanding. Yet for all his austerity he has a love of nature and is one of the great Spanish poets. Poetry is often linked to prayer, because it can hint at experiences that prose cannot describe. John of the Cross illuminates the spiritual night through which many have to pass on the way to deeper fellowship with God, with these lines on the lover and the beloved:

> O night that led'st me thus!
> O night more winsome than the rising sun!
> O night that madest us,
> Lover and lov'd, as one.
> Lover transform'd in lov'd, love's journey done!

Though called to be an enclosed nun, Teresa spent fifteen years journeying about Spain, founding convents of her reformed order, seventeen in all. A papal nuncio, one of her many opponents, called her 'a restless, disobedient, contumacious gad-about'. She travelled with her nuns in old, lumbering covered wagons. Once when they were almost swept away by a river in flood, she said in her prayers: 'No wonder, Lord, you have so few friends, when you treat them so badly like this.' The inns were bug-infested and the nights often icy. Through exhaustion and ill-health she went on and on. Her next book, *Foundations*, tells us of her adventures.

The last large book Teresa wrote is *The Interior Castle* or *The Mansions*, which is about something she cared for even more than the reforming of her order – that is, our closer walk with God. It is a Catholic *Pilgrim's Progress*, the summing up of our lifelong journey to God in authentic prayer. Still she cares for the beginners, who are outside in the cold, damp courtyard with its toads and reptiles. But once inside the castle we can step by step make our way through different 'mansions' or sets of rooms. There isn't a particular number. In the innermost mansion is the King of Glory, but his presence enlightens and beautifies the whole castle. She calls us to strengthen our spiritual muscles. Teresa is feminine, but very virile. She tells her nuns to be strong men.

Her books and her letters are a joy to read. She has to steal time, she says, to write, and adds: 'I wish I could write with both hands so as not to forget one thing while I am saying another.' Out it all pours – digressions, asides, repetitions and even spelling mistakes. All the time she is just herself.

But that is what attracts us – just herself. So human, she wants letters. Feeling old, exhausted on a journey, she asks her beloved director Gracian to write more often, by referring to herself in the third person and to him as 'that gentleman', half shyly, half playfully: 'Beg that gentleman, though he may be careless by nature, not to be so with her; for, where there is love, it cannot slumber so long' (*Letters*, ii. 683).

Earlier in her life she tells us she was always 'very fond of being liked' (*Relations*, iii. (1. 316)). We feel she is still the same, though enriched by the divine love and grace. 'Grace perfects nature.' Her life of prayer, so real, so persevering, so deep, did not separate her from the needs of her neighbours nor diminish her warm humanity.

8

Francis de Sales and Jeanne de Chantal

Never shall I forget standing on the spot where these two friends met for what they called 'the days of our dedication'. She had ridden there through early summer countryside from Dijon – some seven days on horseback – with a small copy of the French psalms as always in her saddlebag for the journey. How she loved the psalms! Here in a great castle he had been born, a two months' premature baby, the eldest of thirteen children,' thirty-eight years before. She was five years younger.

Two castles used to stand where the smiling meadows of Savoy meet the narrow mountain valley d'Usillon with its sheer limestone cliffs – the Château de Sales with its six towers and the smaller Château de Thorens. Only the latter remains. The actual spot where Francis was born is now a chapel beside an old farm. Francis, bishop of this diocese from the shores of the Lake of Geneva to the high snows of Mt Blanc, and the recently-widowed Mme de Chantal walked in the garden and sat and talked for a week. When I was there, all was silent except for the chattering of starlings in the half-dozen tall elms and the swish of house-martins like arrows through the air.

The bishop, although her spiritual guide, shared with her some of the problems of his work. She spoke to him of strange doubts in the heart of her life of prayer. He advised her to try to turn away from them; they were quite involuntary; she was not to write about them, but she could speak about them when they met. All through her life these doubts persisted, but they never hindered her from bringing to others a real *Abba* confidence. She spoke to Francis of her desire to enter a convent, although her family of four were not yet grown up. He replied 'No', and told her that for the present it was possible for her to give herself completely to God through living under harassing conditions, half a year with her father and half a year with her

53

father-in-law, whose dominating housekeeper was also his mistress.

For the feast of Pentecost Francis had to go to his cathedral fifteen miles away at Annecy, but Jeanne de Chantal stayed over the weekend in the château with the bishop's mother, and on the Tuesday morning took the youngest daughter of the house to a convent school in Burgundy. She carried with her a note from the bishop: 'Nothing could possibly separate your soul from mine, the link is too strong; death itself cannot break it because it is fashioned from a substance that lasts to all eternity.'

After his early years in the Château de Sales and his schooling at Annecy, Francis was sent at the age of thirteen with his own servant and a strict priest-tutor to the university of Paris. He studied in a Jesuit college and we shall see the influence of Ignatius on his early writings. But like many students he went through a spell of depression. He felt cut off from God. He couldn't eat, he couldn't sleep. This dark experience of his own he used to help Jeanne de Chantal and others in their distress. Then one day in desperation he went into the church of St Etienne des Grès in the rue St Jacques, and prayed for relief before the statue of the Black Virgin. And the cloud was lifted. (The church is no longer there, but the statue is preserved in a convent nearby.)

He was six years in Paris; and then took brilliant doctorates in law and in theology at Padua. After all these years Francis was welcomed home to the Château de Sales by his father. He had been forty-five at Francis' birth and his wife only fourteen. A formidable character, he had a career planned for his son and a bride ready for him. Francis took no interest in the girl and confided to his mother that his heart was set on becoming a priest. When this news leaked out, his father was furious. But strings were pulled to secure that Francis, as soon as he should be ordained, would be made provost of the cathedral and second only to the bishop. With this the father was pacified – but not for long.

The Chablais, the strip of the diocese on the southern shore of Lake Geneva, had long been Calvinist. But it had now just passed back politically into the hands of the Catholic Duke of Savoy, who called for volunteers to recatholicize it. It would be a hard task, even dangerous to life. To his father's intense annoyance Francis volunteered; and his only companion was a cousin. Every night they had for safety to trudge up a steep hill to the castle of a Catholic nobleman. From the chapel which survives from this Château d'Allinges you can see clearly the lake and Thonon, the capital of Chablais. It was slow work; but perhaps good for Francis who from birth had had things a little too easy.

After four years the tide turned. The Duke was delighted and then sent Francis on a diplomatic journey to Paris. After the chill Calvinism of the Chablais, Paris of 1602 was what he needed with its warm Catholic springtime. People crowded to meet the young priest. Henry IV wished to keep him in Paris and said of him: 'A rare bird, this Monsieur de Genève, devout and learned, and also a gentleman – a very rare combination.' More important for Francis was the way he was drawn into the heart of this spiritual renewal. He knew intimately Père Bérulle, who founded the French Oratory, a community to help priests to follow a deeper and more disciplined life of prayer. He met also Mme Acarie, a devoted wife and very businesslike woman who brought to France the Carmelites of Teresa of Avila; and who after her husband's death herself entered that order.

As he was on his way home, Francis heard that the bishop in Annecy had died and that he was to succeed him. What a change from Paris! Annecy was tiny and provincial. It looked across a small lake to the mountains of Savoy. Its old houses, many built beside narrow flower-decked canals, were still mostly packed within its medieval walls. Francis was, like his predecessor, nominally bishop of Geneva, but that city had become the Mecca of Calvinists. So his cathedral was a dull church in Annecy and his episcopal palace an equally dull house opposite it. But he now had a profound influence by word and by pen. He wrote letters of spiritual counsel, some to a Mme Chamoisy, whose house you can still see by one of those charming canals.

Presently he collected much of this material and in 1608 turned it into his *Introduction to the Devout Life*. Many spiritual books have been written primarily for monks, nuns and hermits, though we can adapt much of their advice to ourselves. But Francis de Sales was the first to write for men and women in the busy world – though his was a cultured, comfortably-off world. 'It is an error, nay rather a heresy,' he said, 'to wish to banish the life of prayer from the army, from the workshop, from the courts of princes, from married households' (*Introduction*, i. 1). He gave definite commensense advice about daily life and clear directions about the ordinary life of prayer. He urged the importance of regular mediation, as Ignatius Loyola did. Like Ignatius again, he speaks of our need of a guide.

But Ignatius wrote in a crabbed Spanish and Francis in an elegant, freely-flowing French. Above all Francis writes from the heart. Love differs from prayer, he wrote, 'no more than flame does from fire'.

Within his lifetime this book was reprinted forty times and translated into English, Italian, Latin, Spanish and German. But before it was published, he was being invited far and wide to preach courses of sermons. One of these was at Dijon in Lent 1604; and it was there in the Sainte Chapelle and in her father's house that he first met, already a widow, Jeanne de Chantal.

Jeanne's mother died before she was two. She was brought up by her father, the president of the parliament of Dijon, whom she adored. To her novices many years later she described herself as 'fille à toute folie': 'ready for any mischief'. She married a young soldier of her father's choice. She was soon head over heels in love. When he was away fighting, she put his estate into order and made it solvent. When he was home, she dressed to please him and didn't spend too long at her prayers. As in the home of any other good Catholic gentleman of that day, there was a daily mass in the château chapel; but to get him there she had on dark mornings to wave a lighted taper close to his eyes to wake him up.

Then one day when out hunting, the young husband was accidentally shot by a friend. For a week he lay in great pain at home dying. She ran out along into the woods, crying out to God: 'Take all I have, my children, everything, but leave me my husband.' He died, and she was a widow at twenty-eight, with four young children under five. In her grief she kept his love in her heart and preserved a love-poem from him all through her years as a nun. For strength she now turned almost ferociously to her religion. By misfortune she put herself under the direction of an over-strict, dominating priest. Her life was hard indeed.

When she began to know Francis, she gradually and reluctantly opened to him her troubles. Equally reluctantly he offered to help. Francis was always slow to come to the point. He heard her confession in that Easter week and agreed to give her more detailed advice when they should meet in August at Saint Claude, a shrine in the Jura mountains about half-way between Dijon and Annecy. But before then, on his journey home from Dijon to Annecy, he sent her a note: 'I think that God gave me to you; every hour makes me more sure.' They met at Saint Claude, he agreed to be her spiritual guide and counselled her along the lines of the *Introduction to the Devout Life*.

With Francis at Annecy, Mme de Chantal found other spiritual help in Dijon itself. Francis approved, he was never jealous. The Carmelites, whom Mme Acarie had brought from Spain, had opened a convent in Dijon. Francis had taught Mme de Chantal to make daily a systematic, fairly reasoned-out meditation. The Carmelites now suggested to her a simpler, less planned, more contemplative way of praying. We can follow Francis' letters to her on this subject. 'Let us continue our systematic meditation as we go along the valley,' was what he first said, 'while those God calls to steeper climbs can practise these simpler ways.' But gradually he himself, the spiritual guide, learnt this more contemplative praying from Jeanne de Chantal and her Carmelite friends.

So Francis watched over her spiritual development and by 1610 he felt the moment had come for them to found together the new contemplative Order of the Visitation for women at Annecy. You can still see outside the city walls by the lake their first house, not much more than a large cottage, with its garden where the bishop came to speak with them. At first they did a little sick visiting, but they were never like Vincent de Paul's Sisters of Charity; rather their primary desire was always to grow in love through contemplative praying.

It was his conversations with them in that garden which helped him to put the last touches in 1616 to his larger, rather diffuse book, *The Treatise on the Love of God*. 'We meditate to awaken love,' he wrote. 'We contemplate, because we love.'

Jeanne de Chantal had helped him to discover this. And now he had to help her to take another step forward. Just before this book came out, she made a retreat alone at Whitsuntide 1616. He was ill at the time, so he had to send notes to her. One contained these enigmatic words: 'Our Lord loves you, my mother: he wants you to be all his. Think no longer about the friendship in which God has joined us, nor about your children, nor about your body, nor your soul, nor indeed anything whatever.' He cannot have meant to unsay anything he had said to her, any more than he wished her to be indifferent to her children. His way was always: '*Tout par amour, rien par force*' – 'all by love, nothing by force'. I can only hazard a guess. She had been dependent – and rightly so – on her father, on her beloved husband and on Francis himself. Now she had to make a step towards her full maturity, her true self, by realizing – whatever encouragement she received through others – her immediate, direct dependence on God. She understood it, she consented by love. That

57

is clearly how her life was now shaped.

In 1618 Francis was in Paris to negotiate the marriage of the Prince of Piedmont to a French princess. Once more every moment of his time was taken. Everyone wanted to hear him preach and to talk with him. Mme de Chantal was also in Paris, founding a convent for her Visitation nuns – first in a ramshackle house, but then in an elegant one in the rue Saint Antoine and with a church, later given by Napoleon to the Protestants. She wrote a little sadly: 'We see our Father from time to time, but it is impossible to talk with him. But God's holy will be done.'

In December 1622 he was in Lyons for the meeting of Louis XIII and the Duke of Savoy. He refused royal hospitality and stayed in a gardener's cottage at the Visitation convent. He was fifty-three, but prematurely worn out. Mme de Chantal was at the convent. She said: 'Father, I have two lists, one about my own spiritual life and the other about the affairs of the community; which shall we talk about?' 'The second,' he replied. 'About the first we will talk when we meet in Annecy.' They never saw each other again. The next day she went to their convent at Grenoble. Three days after Christmas, still in Lyons, he died. When she heard, she passed a day and a night in tears. His body was brought back to Annecy; she prayed long beside it. Then she reverted, with no backward look, to what she called her *façon ordinaire*, 'her usual manner'. She worked and prayed incessantly. She became the architect of their steadily-growing community and also a blessing to thousands outside. Although she still had to contend with her inner doubts, people said of her, 'To be with you strengthens my faith.'

9

Vincent de Paul and Louise de Marillac

Louise de Marillac wrote on 5 June 1627 to Vincent de Paul: 'Allow me, Father, to importune you again on the subject of a village girl, aged twenty-eight, whom they wish to bring from Burgundy to give herself to me.' Who would have thought that this was the beginning of a network of social service extending from abandoned babies to hardened criminals? France was then a land of abject poverty and of ostentatious wealth, a country plagued by civil war and pestilence.

She was thirty-six, widowed two years before, unstable, almost neurotic. Vincent de Paul, about ten years older, had been a scheming, ambitious young priest. But his philanthropic achievements these next thirty years – much more aided by her than people used to think – were so amazing that when he was canonized as St Vincent de Paul, even Voltaire exclaimed, 'Now, I have a saint in heaven!' Voltaire was wrong in thinking that Vincent was primarily a philanthropist. He was very deep in prayer; and so was Louise de Marillac. Prayer involved leaving the world for the Desert Fathers and for Mother Julian; and from them we can learn something. But for ninety-nine per cent of us prayer means prayer where we are – and true prayer makes us more where we are. And this means sustained effort and discipline.

Ignatius was born in a castle south of the Pyrenees; a hundred years later Vincent was running barefoot on a small farm north of the Pyrenees. He was a quick-witted lad, and his father sold a yoke of oxen to send the boy to the university of Toulouse. Then the snobbish student refused to see his father when he came to visit him. When he was ordained Vincent, not wishing to be an impoverished village priest, set up a school for the better-off. A thief disappeared with some of his money and he tracked him down to Marseilles. As he was coming back part of the way by sea, his boat was seized by Turkish pirates and he found himself being paraded before the buyers in a slave-market at Tunis before passing into the hands of a lapsed Christian with three wives. Through one of these women he persuaded his master to return to Savoy. Eventually at Avignon the man was reconciled to the church by a papal legate, who took a liking to Vincent and brought him to Rome. There Vincent made the most of his contacts; so much so, that Pope Paul v entrusted him with a confidential message to Henry iv of France. In Paris he contrived to secure a post at the court of Queen Marguerite of Valois.

But far more important, he took as his guide Père de Bérulle who, as we have seen, was at the heart of a spiritual renewal in France. We wish we knew more of what passed between these two men, but one result was that Vincent did hospital visiting. There he cared for a priest, a doctor of theology at the Sorbonne and formerly a violently anti-Protestant controversialist. This man had now lost his faith and was threatening suicide. Vincent prayed and ministered to him in vain; then he offered to take this darkness upon himself, if only the man could be cured. The theologian regained his faith. But Vincent himself was now plunged for three or four months in doubt and anguish. Then Vincent declared to God that, if he in turn could be restored to faith, he would consecrate the rest of his life to the service of the underprivileged. His doubts vanished, never to return.

Encouraged by Père de Bérulle, he went as parish priest to Clichy, then a poor, small town on the outskirts of Paris. There Vincent found himself. 'I am more happy than I can express,' he said to the Cardinal Archbishop of Paris. 'Neither his Holiness the Pope nor you, your Eminence, could be as happy as I am.'

After two years de Bérulle made the extraordinary decision to send this priest, who had so recently consecrated himself to the service of the poor, to be chaplain to the de Gondi family with their immense wealth. M de Gondi was general of the galleys and the lieutenant-general of the King's fleet in the Levant. Mme de Gondi was beautiful and pious. Their children, whose tutor Vincent was to be, were known as 'the three young devils'. He may not have been able to do much good for them, but he soon had a great influence with their parents. As he moved with the family from one of their great estates to another, his eyes were opened to the ignorance – and worse – of people and clergy in the countryside. He developed a method of conducting missions, and so he discovered another of his great gifts. But still he felt imprisoned, he said, 'in a golden cage'.

Once when the family was away, he disappeared and again became an ordinary parish priest at Châtillon-les-Dombes near Lyons. In no time he won the hearts of his parishioners, Calvinists as well as Catholics, and found out how to organize the care of the poor by the rich; in fact he set up the first of his Confraternities of Charity. But a barrage of letters from the de Gondis and a few words from Père de Bérulle dragged him back to 'the golden cage'. They extracted a promise from him that he would never desert them again. They and he were about the same age and it looked as if he was there for life.

True, there were compensations. He was in close touch with the great world of Paris, men and women of wealth who soon became patrons of new Confraternities of Charity. There too he met Francis de Sales and Mme de Chantal, and he was asked by Francis de Sales to become his friend's spiritual guide. Vincent began to organize a company of priests and to conduct missions. Then unexpectedly Mme de Gondi died, and her husband gave up his riches and became a priest in the oratory of Père de Bérulle. Now at forty-five Vincent was free and his real life began – and just then Louise de Marillac crossed his path.

The illegitimate daughter of a nobleman, Louise never knew a mother's love. Very early she was placed in the royal convent of Poissy, where her aunt was a nun. There she received a cultured education. She set her heart on entering the very austere order of the Capuchines, who had just been established in Paris – in fact she made a private vow to do so. But they would not receive her, probably rightly, as she did not have the necessary physical strength or nervous stability. For her, as for Teresa of Avila and women of their class, it was either marriage or a convent. No nobleman would marry her on account of her birth – and this would have to be declared publicly in her marriage contract – but the de Marillac family found for her an up-and-coming young man of the bourgeoisie, M le Gras, a secretary to Queen Marie de Medici. So Louise became known as Mlle le Gras, as the term Madame was then reserved to wives of the nobility.

It was an arranged marriage, but they were soon in love, lived affluently and within a year had a son. She had as her confessor Jean Pierre Camus, Bishop of Belley, a close friend of Francis de Sales. Then M le Gras became ill and peevish. She was depressed and worried because she had not fulfilled her adolescent vow to become a nun. She considered leaving her husband. She doubted the reality of God and the future life. But during mass at Pentecost 1623 she had a divine intuition that all was well, that she should remain with her husband and also – unwelcome to her – that she would have to change her confessor. Louise settled down to tenderly nursing her husband until he died at the end of 1625; and all through her life she spoke of him as *mon bon mari*, my dear husband.

The change of confessor meant going to Vincent de Paul. Both hesitated. She would miss Bishop Camus' charm, and Vincent perhaps feared that she might become another tie to him like Mme de Gondi. Vincent's first letters to her were cool, though Vincent could not write to anyone as Francis de Sales used to write. Anyway, she soon felt dependent, perhaps too dependent, on Vincent. She could not stand it when he left Paris without letting her know. Bishop Camus saw what was happening and wrote: 'As soon as M Vincent is out of sight, Mlle le Gras is in despair.' But before long Vincent was writing to her more warmly. He asks her to tell no one about his attacks of fever, but then adds, 'My heart could not conceal it from you'. Again he writes that he knows he has, after her son, the first place in her prayers.

Vincent soon began to recognize Louise's abilities and her need to be drawn out of herself. He sent her, despite her frail health, all over France, by coach, by barge and on horseback, in the heat of summer and in the frosts of winter, to supervise his Confraternities of Charity. This demanded business ability, discernment and wisdom. For the lords and ladies who had given their services were often haughty, and the priests sometimes jealous. It was a great achievement and she grew in confidence. And when she was in Paris, Vincent also entrusted her with the responsibility of guiding these aristocratic ladies in their private retreats, using outlines like those of Ignatius Loyola.

But more important still, he sent to live with her in her home rough country girls who had been touched by the missions of his confrères. These young women would never do for the convent life of that day. But they were exactly the women to nurse the poor who were in the care of his confraternities. Before long they were rescuing abandoned children, giving elementary education, attending to the utterly neglected insane, reforming filthy overcrowded hospitals, helping prisoners who were destined to be galley-slaves. This was virtually the first time nuns had been seen outside their cloisters. It was a religious revolution. People said these girls would never manage it, they would be cheated and raped. The young widow succeeded in training them for this almost impossible task; and above all she convinced them that the inexhaustible love they would need could only spring out of deep, regular prayer.

At the same time Vincent and his brother priests were conducting missions all over France with astonishing results. He told them that at home they must be as prayerful as Carthusians in order to be apostles out of doors. But he realized that many of their missions would be only 'a flash in the pan', unless the parish priests were capable of maintaining the new spiritual impetus; and many were not. He arranged regular conferences for the clergy every Tuesday in his community house. He gave special and long retreats before the ordination of young priests. But he was sure that he must go further back into their training, and so his company themselves set up seminaries; and he said to those in charge, 'As a sword is to a soldier, so is prayer to a priest.'

No longer was Vincent ambitious. 'Never go ahead of God's providence,' he used to say; but added that once we know what we are to do, then there must be no let-up. By this time everybody knew Vincent. He was at the death-bed of Louis XIII. He became confessor to his widow, Anne of Austria. She appointed him as a member of a royal council to advise about the choice of bishops. He deliberated with elegant courtiers. When they complained of his old, worn-out cassock, green with age, he replied, 'It's patched, but it's clean'. In all his growing responsibilities he was just himself.

He lived to be eighty. Louise de Marillac died a few months before him. In their last years both still lived in real simplicity, he with his company, she with her Sisters of Charity. Every morning both rose with their companions at four o'clock. They all started with an hour of meditative prayer. Each day was for both of them an almost incessant round of correspondence, of counselling and of service. They found their strength – and their love – in their unfailing prayer, day by day.

Almost to the very end Vincent made time once a week to go and talk with Louise and her Sisters. He, like them, was a peasant. They, sitting round him, were not afraid to put their questions to him. We can still read the accounts of their artless conversations. His peasant's sense of humour and dislike of all humbug is quite clear. There would never be a trace of artificiality or patronage in their service, he told them, as long as they saw and loved the Lord himself in the person they were helping. Mother Teresa says the same in Calcutta today. But how hard it is just to do this. Vincent said that we shall never recognize the Lord in our neighbour unless we have come to know the Lord intimately in our prayer.

These peasant girls say that they find it hard to get up at four. He replies that sometimes he does himself, but he adds that this is their way of showing how essential prayer is. Without regularity, without effort, they will not grow in their love of God. Yet if at that early morning hour they are called to the sick, they are to go at once, and to remember that they are going from God to God.

He calls everyone to meditative prayer – of one kind or another. But no one must become so absorbed by meditative prayer that they think that they can leave behind saying ordinary prayers – intercessions and the corporate prayers of the church. Their meditative prayer may – for even the hardest workers – become simple, more wordless, more contemplative. As Vincent sits with Louise and these country girls, he asks: 'And how do you know that God doesn't want to make a Teresa out of you?'

10

Henry Vaughan and Awareness

It is as difficult to write about prayer, as it is about love; for love is too deep for words, and so is prayer. How then can you begin to convey to others what love or prayer is? Is the Zen saying here true – 'He who knows doesn't speak, and he who speaks doesn't know'? Yes, I think so; but the words of the poet can do something, even if prose can't. For poetry – or at least the kind of poetry I have in mind and this includes some of Henry Vaughan's lines – doesn't describe, but hints at, real experience. And this experience in prayer, I am going to call 'awareness'. It is not just thinking about God, nor is it merely emotion. It is something solid and deep, not describable, but it can be hinted at and perhaps communicated through this creative language and other arts. Vaughan wrote in 'The Morning Watch':

> Prayer is
> The world in tune,
> A spirit-voice,
> And vocal joys
> Whose echo is heaven's bliss.

What starts off as definition is not even description. What are we to do with lines like these?

Most of our books about prayer are prosy. Maybe they aren't even really about prayer. Prayer is something like the incandescent gas between the two electric poles of a strip-lighting tube. How I dislike these analogies, and specially impersonal ones – but how else can one talk?

Many books on spirituality are not about the incandescent gas at all, they are about one of the two poles – they are either about the nature of God, disclosed to us in Jesus and coming to us in the

Holy Spirit; or else they are about the nature of man, made marvellously capable of fellowship with God, yet spoilt, but now able to be restored. Other spiritual books are about techniques – 'teach-yourself-to-pray' – often quite useful in their place; but these books correspond only to the little 'starter', which inside the tube builds up the necessary difference of potential between the two poles. But what we are really looking for is some writing not about the poles, nor about the starter, but about the incandescent gas itself which radiates the light.

Let us take a better analogy, a personal one, human friendship and love in their many forms. There are books about men and women, their psychology and potentialities. There are also 'teach-yourself' books, on how to build up personal relationships. But none of these is what we are looking for at this moment; we want to know what 'awareness' in friendship and love is really like. This is how some poets can help us; they can hint to us what it is like to experience human friendship and love – and also what it is like to experience fellowship with God in prayer and in life. Thomas Merton, you remember, says that a good poem 'induces an experience'. Some lines of Henry Vaughan do this rather as some verses of the psalms can.

In 1622, the year Francis de Sales died in Lyons, Henry Vaughan and his twin brother were born in the tiny hamlet of Newton among the rolling hills of South Wales. About five miles from the nearest town of Brecon, his house still stands beside the road. As a boy he must often have climbed the Allt, the hill behind the house. He would look across the green, farming valley with its meandering river Usk to the Brecon Beacons, half as high as Snowdon. Almost all his life he lived here as a doctor; and many times he must have watched the sun piercing the white clouds and gilding little patches of the opposite hillside, as in these lines from 'Regeneration';

> The unthrift sun shot vital gold
> A thousand pieces
> And heaven its azure did unfold
> Chequered with snowy fleeces.

The brothers rode together beside the Usk, then over the narrow twelve-arched Crickhowell bridge to Llangattock for their schooling. They enjoyed their lessons with the village priest-schoolmaster in his rectory beside the massive pink sandstone church tower. Later they went on like many Welshmen to Jesus College, Oxford. Thomas was eventually ordained and became a fellow of his college. Henry did not take his degree but went to study law in London and presumably medicine. He admits he found himself in an idle, showy set. He returned home and was soon a practising doctor. His twin brother became the parish priest of Llansantffraed, a mile from home. The civil war broke out and both brothers fought on the Royalist side. They suffered defeat. Thomas, like other Anglican clergy, was deprived of his living by the Puritans. By this time Henry had written *Olor Iscanus* (Swan of the Usk), some Cavalier poetry of no great merit, including some love-poems to the girl who was to be his first wife. His next book of poems, *Silex Scintillans* (Sparks of the Flint), was altogether different. Clearly something had happened to him; it was his conversion. How it came about we do not know, except that it was, he said, through the influence of 'Mr George Herbert, whose holy life and verse gained many pious converts, of whom I am the least'.

Herbert was from an aristocratic family on the Welsh borders; he had a distinguished career at Cambridge, but then gave up everything to become an Anglican parish priest. He ministered like a saint for three years in the tiny church of Bemerton, almost within sight of the elegant spire of Salisbury. He died in 1630 at the age of thirty-seven. He published nothing during his lifetime, but from his death-bed he sent to his friend, Nicholas Ferrar, the leader of an extended-family community at Little Gidding near Cambridge, a small collection of his highly-polished verse, *The Temple*. These poems fell into the hands of Henry Vaughan and transformed both his life and his writing. Herbert made Vaughan more of a poet, but not, as is sometimes said, after his own image. The lay-out of their poems is so alike. But how very different the men are. George Herbert is the priest before the altar. Henry Vaughan is a man of the open air, a doctor riding over the Welsh hills – and often beneath the night stars, which spoke so clearly to him. For him as for Wordsworth

> Kind nature keeps a heavenly door
> Wide open.

Vaughan writes about this change in his life in the poem, 'Regeneration', near the beginning of his first edition of *Silex Scintillans* in 1650. Five years later he brought out a much larger edition. Vaughan sees himself climbing on to his Welsh hills in spring 'all the way primrosed'. But he himself was still 'frost within'. It was a hard climb 'rough-cast with rocks'. At the top he found strangely enough a pair of scales set up, meaning I think that he had to weigh up between the delusive pleasures of life and a serious search for God. He decided; 'straight I obeyed'. Then he goes resolutely on his journey, like Bunyan's pilgrim. At last he hears the rushing wind of the Spirit:

> Lord, then said I, On me one breath,
> And let me die before my death.

In New Testament words, 'Dying, and behold we live'; as we let ourselves die to our lower self, we come alive to the true life, the eternal life here and now. Conversion happens – and goes on.

So Vaughan went on, ever a seeker. He had no easy life. His wife died, he married again, the families quarrelled, there was litigation; he and his second wife had to give up their home and live in a cottage, but still within the sound of his beloved river Usk. After a life of service among those Welsh hills and many years of quiet, reflective seeking of God, he was buried by Llansantffraed church. Through the branches of yew trees you can see the glint of the river and still read his epitaph:

> Unprofitable servant, Greatest of sinners
>
> Glory – Mercy

As a poet Vaughan hints at and perhaps conveys to us the awareness of God. He does not reason with us, he does not set up to teach us, he shares this awareness with us – often in a glowing line or two, quite unexpected. That is his supreme gift. He can't write the beautiful, structured – and rather authoritarian – poems of George Herbert. In my opinion Henry Vaughan doesn't write much really good verse. Sometimes I find him tedious. But every now and again he sparks off glowing lines – and what lines they are.

I would like to leave you to discover your own treasured lines of Vaughan – and then you will treasure them more. Let me share a few of my discoveries to start you on your search. Here is real paradox and striking alliteration:

> There is in God (some say)
> A deep, but dazzling darkness.

Or see him grasping at the transcendental:

> I saw Eternity the other night
> Like a great ring of pure and endless light.

Two seminal lines for me and perhaps for you:

> But life is, what none can express,
> A quickness which my God hath kiss'd.

And of death – so thin is the veil to him – he can write, 'Dear beauteous death'. Such lines are like the sparks which, in Vaughan's day, were struck by a pair of flints to kindle a light.

How can we treasure and walk in the light which he has kindled for us? This is what is meant I think by the New Testament phrase – 'pondering his words in our hearts'. Or more simply, how do close friends treasure one another's words and keep them ringing in their memories? We need to find out how to do this with Vaughan's lines, both in some of our quiet times set aside for prayer, and also in special moments – oases of remembrance – in our busy days. This is a way to be drawn into a growing fellowship with God. This divine fellowship – again like friendship and love – we experience not as an achievement but as a gift given. How can we keep ourselves open to receive this gift through the Spirit?

Henry Vaughan would not have had these moments of inspired awareness, I think, without his regular daily pattern of prayer. He writes of his need of this so often. He speaks of his night prayers as 'My soul's calm retreat, which none disturb'. And in the morning, when 'the quick world awakes and sings', he joins his praises to 'the great chime and symphony of nature'. In his prose work, *The Mount of Olives*, we can read actual prayers he prayed at these times and also in the busy practice of a doctor's life.

He loved the scriptures: 'Welcome dear book, soul's joy and food,' and he prays, 'O that I had deep cut in my hard heart each line in thee.' This quiet kind of reflection is implied, I think, by the context of these lines: 'I walked the other day – to spend my hour – into a field.' Some of his long, scriptural poems look like meditations written out. Professor Louis Martz of Yale produces some evidence that instructions on meditation by Ignatius Loyola and Francis de Sales were circulating among these Anglican men of prayer of the seventeenth century. Certainly we know that *The Introduction to the Devout Life* was bound by Nicholas Ferrar's domestic bindery at Little Gidding.

Yet Vaughan knew – as perhaps we do – the dark valleys as well as the fresh hilltops of the daily life of prayer. Sometimes he feels a void in these 'morning-meetings' and 'evening-walks' and he complains

> Why is my God thus slow and cold,
> When I am most, most sick and sad?

But he knows the secret of perseverance. 'Love only can with lively access unlock the way.'

This love was for him nourished in many ways and particularly through the sacrament in his village church – 'Welcome sweet and sacred feast; welcome life.' Of course, this sacrament was in his days celebrated by Anglicans infrequently, and not at all – unless secretly – during the years under Cromwell. Nowadays nearly all Christians come to holy communion more frequently and with a wider understanding of it, but – how often loss goes with gain – perhaps with much less real devotion.

> Then kneel my soul, and body; kneel and bow;
> If saints and angels fall down, much more thou.

Henry Vaughan spent three days in preparation for receiving the sacrament, meditating on passages from the New Testament. During the day after receiving it, he says we should specially be 'instant in prayer, meditations, thanksgiving and good works' and he adds characteristically, 'not only for a day or two'.

Kneeling at the sacrament in his village church by the rippling Usk helped to give Vaughan awareness of God as he rode over his Welsh hills beneath the stars, busy in his calling as a doctor.

I I

Jean-Pierre de Caussade and the
Present Moment

The greatest difficulty in the life of prayer for many modern people
is the relentless pressure on our time. It is not a new problem.
Ignatius Loyola, Teresa of Avila, Francis de Sales, Vincent de Paul
and those who helped them all knew it. It only happens to be more
widespread in our time. How well I know it myself. My life is tightly –
and enjoyably – packed with travelling, speaking, seeing people and
writing.

The man who has helped me most is an obscure eighteenth-cen-
tury French priest, Jean-Pierre de Caussade. He was so little known
that no one dreamt of attributing to him the only book he published
– anonymously. And the book which we can now buy cheaply in
paperback consists of retreat notes which someone came across a
hundred years after Père de Caussade died. This is the little spiritual classic, *Self-Abandonment to Divine Providence*. It is a book for
us to read and return to again and again, like turning on our journey
towards a true friend whose wisdom and experience are there to help
us. Not only when the way has been 'rough-cast with rocks' but
during everyday walks has de Caussade helped me to take things one
at a time and not be irritated or overwhelmed by them.

He was born in the south of France in 1675, twenty years before
Henry Vaughan died. He was for fourteen years a Jesuit school-
master, never long at any school and teaching in turn almost all the
subjects of the curriculum. Next he was put on to giving missions
like Vincent de Paul's mission priests. Then he conducted retreats
in Lorraine and was spiritual guide in Nancy to some of the
Visitation Sisters, founded by Jeanne de Chantal.

He himself wrote like Francis de Sales; he was sensitive to each
person. And his teaching was no abstract theology, but warm with
his own experience of love and prayer. He said in one of his letters

that he felt *investi d'une mission*, called to share with others the particular message and insight entrusted to him by God.

Then he fell into disrepute. We don't know exactly why. But to the disappointment of the Sisters he was suddenly recalled to the south of France and had to live for a time in a seminary at Albi. In a letter to one of the nuns he said he was trembling at the consequences of some imprudent words he had spoken. I think he may have been suspected of encouraging 'quietism' in some of those who sought his advice.

Briefly speaking, the 'quietists' of the seventeenth century were genuinely drawn towards quiet, receptive, contemplative praying, which we have referred to several times in this book; but unfortunately they went on further to make unbalanced statements about the life of prayer. The pendulum in all ages easily swings too far. The 'quietists' were rightly convinced that contemplative praying, however much we may desire it, seek it and open ourselves to receive it, is in the end truly a gift which we receive from God passively – or apparently quite passively. But then they made the extravagant and unbalanced deduction that those other forms of prayer, which require active human effort, like systematic intercessions or straightforward reflection on the scriptures, become eventually unnecessary for us. Clearly their views were contrary to the Bible and the Christian tradition.

Among those condemned for their 'quietism' were Miguel de Molinos, a Spanish priest; Mme Guyon, a widow close to the court of Louis XIV; and also, though much less so, Fénelon, Archbishop of Cambrai. But Bossuet, Bishop of Meaux, a gifted preacher, spoke out against them. There was tense controversy all over France. Some of the Jesuits seemed to sniff out 'quietism' everywhere. So de Caussade may have fallen under the suspicion of some of his confrères. However, after two years he was restored to his post at Nancy, to the joy of the nuns. It was at this time that he published anonymously his book, *Spiritual Instructions on Prayer*, with the tactful sub-title 'Various Stages of Prayer according to the Doctrine of Bossuet, Bishop of Meaux'. In this book de Caussade maintained – perhaps with a little special pleading – that Bossuet condemned not 'quietists' themselves, but only their extravagances.

Later Père de Caussade was made superior of two Jesuit houses in succession. This was a recognition of his value, though it was no great claim to fame, because there were thousands of Jesuit houses. It was a responsibility he disliked and wrote about with wry humour. Finally he returned to the mother house at Toulouse and died at the age of seventy-five after being blind for some years and bearing it courageously.

To me the most arresting phrase from his book of retreat notes, *Self-Abandonment to Divine Providence*, is 'the sacrament of the present moment'. I am sure that I have not fathomed its full depth yet.

Père de Caussade builds everything on the New Testament disclosure that God's very nature is love, unchangeable love. 'God is love' – not a soft love, but a challenging and transforming love. God is therefore loving each one of us every instant of our lives, for he can no more stop loving us than the sun can stop radiating heat. It follows, de Caussade says, that God's love is somehow coming to us through each single moment, through what is happening just now. His love can't reach us now through what happened yesterday or what will happen next week, but through what we are doing and experiencing at this moment.

'Why should not', Père de Caussade then asks, 'every moment of our lives be a sort of communion with the divine love?' For God intends his love to reach us not only through the holy sacrament – although the holy sacrament meant so much to him, as it did to Henry Vaughan, and de Caussade would never minimize what it can mean to us. But, he declares – as a Quaker like Rufus Jones might say – 'God makes of all things mysteries and sacraments of his love.' But how can we train ourselves – and it needs training – to receive this 'sacrament of the present moment'? Two things are required.

First, we need to become deeply rooted in this basic conviction that God is love. We glanced earlier in our chapter on John at the fundamental New Testament grounds for this conviction. I realize that there are also even deeper questions to be faced, such as 'Is God real?' and 'How can Jesus be divine as well as human?' I have already looked at these problems in a book of mine, *Dynamic of Love*, and I hope before long to be able to write about them at greater length.

Père de Caussade himself recalls us to this New Testament conviction and invites us to reflect on its implications for ourselves. 'Did the Lord not prove that he loved us more than life itself, since he laid down his life for us? And can we then not be assured that having done so much he will never forget us?' But intellectual reflection, important as it is, will not give us all that we need. In the

73

life of prayer as in our daily responsibilities we need to harness our other personal resources, besides our intellect. What family life, what friendships, could flourish on intellect alone?

So we come back again to the vital importance of meditation. Louis Martz, whom I mentioned a few pages ago, says in effect that meditation begins with the interpenetration of our genuine intellectual analysis by our sense of wonder and love.[1] Then the conviction that God is love will gradually permeate our whole personality. And these times of meditative praying will become increasingly times when we expose ourselves to this ever-present love of God and when we can express more and more the response of our love and our confidence in him. This will not always be 'plain sailing', any more than human friendship and love are. But we know we need frequently to express our affection for one another and to have time for one another. And so it is with this love of God.

The second thing we need, if we are to receive this 'sacrament of the present moment', is the art of concentration, not an easy art in the world of today. We have to train ourselves how to approach each present moment just as it comes – the complicated letter to be written, the misunderstanding to be straightened out, the stranger to be welcomed, the chore to be finished. It is difficult, but we know it can be done, because sometimes we do it. For example, at the moment of receiving holy communion we have sometimes experienced what it is to be absorbed in it and oblivious to everything else. Or when gripped by a book or lost in a piece of writing, we forget clocks and meals and everything else. Or even more clearly when we meet a close friend again after a long absence, hours have gone by before we know where we are. So we have the capacity of concentration; we only need to cultivate it. And when we have done so, we are going to be less anxious men and women and less exhausted.

This is what de Caussade recommends: 'We must cut off all more distant views, we must confine ourselves to the duty of the present moment without thinking of what preceded it or what will follow it.' And he gives his reason: 'The duties of each moment are shadows beneath which the divine action lies concealed.' We must not misunderstand de Caussade. He does not mean us to be careless about the future or improvident, but only not to be anxious about it. Sometimes it is an important duty to plan for the future, and at those moments planning for the future is itself the duty of the present moment. This is how he puts it in one of his delightful letters: 'Try not to let apprehension about the future or regret about the past flood over into your present living and make you miserable.' And isn't this what Jesus said? He didn't tell us not to be concerned with the future, but not to be 'anxious' about the future. And his *Abba* prayer of intimacy and trust enabled him to live this way. The test of all methods of Christian prayer is this: How far do they open us to the Holy Spirit so that he can enable us to participate in the *Abba* prayer of Jesus?

Père de Caussade is realistic and warns us that we are going to find this kind of praying and living hard work, with its concentrating on the present and not being anxious for the future. One of the attractive things about him is that he lets us see how difficult he found it to follow his own advice. In a letter to a nun at Nancy he told her how he had become superior of a Jesuit house at Perpignan with all its unwelcome responsibilities. First he said he grumbled, and complained that he had no aptitude for the job. When he actually arrived, it was even worse than he anticipated. It involved all kinds of business which he could not understand. He also disliked VIP visits: yet the bishop, steward, king's lieutenant, sheriff, garrison officer all called on him. But afterwards – to his own surprise – he could write: 'I remain calm and in peace in the midst of a thousand worries and complications in which I should have expected to be overwhelmed.'

What he asks us to aim at is not a reluctant resignation to the all-but-inevitable, but rather a trustful and wholeheartedly placing of ourselves into the hands of God. This is what the word abandon means in the French title of his book. He sees the supreme example of this self-giving in Mary, the Lord's mother, when she put herself into God's hands, cost what it may, to carry out his great purpose for her: 'Behold, the handmaid of the Lord; be it unto me according to thy word.' There was no nervous fear and no narrowing down of her life; on the contrary, it was 'something very glorious', which ran afterwards like a thread of gold through all 'occupations, commonplace or lofty', of her life.

I would like you to read this short work for yourself. Neither this nor any other book will be 'exactly right' for you. I mentioned earlier that we should follow no guide blindly. To show you what I mean, I've jotted down four of my reactions to de Caussade. He is certainly far beyond me, and I may have misunderstood him.

First, I find it much harder than he does to be sure always what God's will for us is. It was clear enough for Mary at her annunciation; but it is not often like that. Perhaps we should help one another to wrestle with this question.

Secondly, I have some difficulty with his words 'crosses sent by Providence', a phrase used by other writers, both Catholic and Protestant. These hard things come upon us, by no means always through our fault; and, as I have said before, I cannot affirm that they are directly sent by God; though I believe that, if I am growing to love God, he can somehow bring good out of them for others and for me.

Thirdly, de Caussade and many other writers on prayer seem to me to take too negative a view of our human senses and feelings. Perhaps because we live after Freud and Jung we are more perceptive about this. But de Caussade wrote: 'We must kill our senses and be stripped of them; their destruction means the reign of faith.' There may be a grain of truth in this. We may, for example, as *The Cloud of Unknowing* says, have to let our human affections temporarily slip into the 'cloud of forgetting' to have a tranquil openness to God, just as a surgeon may have to 'sterilize' his feelings during an operation for the good of the patient. At any rate I cannot see this killing of the senses in Jesus, neither in his preaching nor in his ceaseless caring for others.

Yet, fourthly, I find de Caussade in general a very encouraging writer. He is very human. There is no hardness nor aloofness in his writing, particularly in his letters. 'Don't worry,' he says about little falls; 'they are permitted in order to help us to practise humility and patience and to endure ourselves. Our falls, seen in this way, will be far more useful to us than victories that are spoiled by vain complacency.' His method is 'accessible to everybody', he says, and fundamentally it adds up to doing with true love the ordinary things our life expects of us moment by moment.

12

Rufus Jones and Today's World

The Nobel Peace Prize was awarded to Rufus Jones in 1947 as the architect of the immense Quaker relief organization after the two world wars. It was the Quaker experience of prayer that gave him both the wisdom and the energy for this enormous task.

In two other ways he was a pioneer. First, he faced up to the questions put to us by the modern historical approach to the scriptures, and showed that historical study made them not less but more valuable for meditation and quiet prayer. Secondly, his grasp of what was then the 'new psychology' brought him to understand more deeply experiences of prayer and mysticism.

So this American Quaker is important for us, because he helps us to look from another angle at our long tradition of prayer.

His ancestors, probably first generation Quakers, came from Wales while Henry Vaughan was still alive. Rufus was born in a remote village in Maine, blanketed by a long snow. His aunt took the baby in her arms and foretold that he should carry 'the gospel to distant lands'. It was a close-knit affectionate family, who worked their own small farm. His grandmother, smoking her long clay pipe, told sagas of the hard pioneering days. Rufus Jones used to say, 'I wasn't christened in a church, but I was sprinkled from morning to night with the dew of grace'; and he was convinced that 'the greatest single help to the spiritual life is a deep, human love for one another'. The Bible was their one book but he said they read it 'as a scholar uses his library'. Twice a week the four-wheeled wagon was brought out to take them through the woods to the Quaker meeting. He was full of mischief and energy. 'I always used to run,' he said, 'because I hadn't time to walk.' He was intelligent too.

In 1879 he went away to a co-ed school – the Quakers were always progressive in that way – and for the first time in his life he travelled by train and boat; he was sixteen. He soon wrote home to say that he had just heard the astonishing fact that this world was not made in six days.

Within a few years he was writing a thesis – a sign of things to come – on 'Mysticism and its Exponents', while an undergraduate at Haverford. This was near Philadelphia, once the city of William Penn and then the haven of dyed-in-the-wool Quakers. Some of them were deeply set in their Thee's and Thou's and every kind of unchangeableism. He started, even as early as this, his life-task of persuading them to accept the new understanding of the scriptures. He had already decided, he said, to throw in his lot 'with the discoverer and creator and not with the conformist'. A few years after taking his degree, he refused a chance of going to Harvard and returned to Haverford where he taught philosophy and much else for over thirty years. Haverford is an attractive place to an Englishman, with its trees and cricket field; and I have worked in what was Rufus Jones' study, now a library of books on mysticism.

Before becoming a professor at Haverford he had taught in a Quaker school. Leaving at the end of a term, he said 'Goodbye' to a girl teacher. Then for some unknown reason he went back, found the girl in tears and in his impulsive, affectionate way proposed to her on the spot. It had to be a long engagement. He was due to go to Europe to perfect his French and German. While walking alone through the woods at Dieulefit, in the foothills of the French Alps, he had the first of his moments of a special sense of God's presence. I do not doubt that these moments were, as it were, the crest of the wave in that daily flow of his Quaker discipline of prayer. He felt, he said, 'the walls between the visible and invisible grow thin'. He knelt down, and heard an inward call to give himself to explore the prayer of quiet and its consequences in life, as clearly as Francis of Assisi at St Damiano was called 'to rebuild the church of God'; and Rufus dedicated himself to God and this call.

He returned to the States and was married. They moved together to another school for a short time. Their son Lowell was born. But before then, another world opened to him: he never forgot how in summer time, lying on the grass under the trees, he opened the pages of William James' *Principles of Psychology*. Rufus Jones quickly realized the light this book would throw on his study of prayer, though psychology has of course since moved on a long way. After eleven years of married happiness his wife died, leaving Lowell just seven, the apple of his father's eye.

Soon Rufus married again. He was invited with his wife to visit the Quakers in England. They left Lowell behind with friends. On the last night of their voyage Rufus had his second vivid experience of God's presence; he felt himself 'surrounded and fortified by an enfolding presence'. The next day they received a cable that Lowell had died after a two-day illness. Rufus was shattered, but was so inwardly strengthened by his experience that he was able to go straight ahead with a series of eleven lectures.

As the years went by, his work kept mounting up. He wrote, for example, five out of seven large volumes of a history of Quakerism. After the First World War he was engaged on the Quaker relief work in France, Germany, Austria and Poland. Not surprisingly he seemed in the early twenties to be heading towards a nervous break-down, and then had a serious street accident. In hospital he received the third of these special experiences of God's presence and power. He felt new spiritual resources welling up within him like, he said, the rising of the level of a great river when there have been heavy rains in the mountains. He became a new man, and a fresh balance and vitality stayed with him all through his last twenty-five years. Right at the end of his life he one day watched a cricket match at Haverford and the next day he died while correcting in bed the proofs of his last book, *A Call to what is Vital*, commending the life of prayer to critically-minded people of our own day.

I have tried to avoid the word 'mysticism', because it is so easily misunderstood. Yet Rufus Jones continually uses it, but he means by it I think something like what I have called quiet, receptive praying, which from time to time can rise to a crest in these moments when God's presence is specially realized. What he says is worth consider-ing because of his particular standpoint as a modern Quaker.

This quiet prayer, he insists, is never more than one part of the Christian's calling and never its chief aim. In particular intellec-tual study should never lose its importance. 'The present-day revolt from doctrine is', he maintains, 'in many ways superficial.' Nor is there only one road to quiet prayer, he says, any more than there is only one approach to human friendship and love. These special moments of the realization of God's presence are not to make us 'unworldly' but – in his own words – 'to clarify life, to give it direc-tion and power'. The whole life of prayer should lead, he said, to an increase 'in the unity and coherence of the personality and in its creative energy'.

In his study of mysticism – and here his knowledge of psychology helps him – he distinguishes three things.[1] First, there is mystical experience which is what we receive from God in quiet prayer and in these special moments. This he maintains is too profound for words; as Mother Julian said, 'I can never fully tell it.' Secondly, there are mystical phenomena, what Germans call *Mystizismus* – visions, voices, trances. These things happen and sometimes bring great insight, as they did to Teresa of Avila. But on the other hand they sometimes seem to be reactions of disordered personalities. Rufus Jones is critical of these phenomena. And so was John of the Cross, saying that at best they are only unessential accompaniments of mystical experience and that they should not be sought for their own sake. Thirdly, there is mystical theology, which tries, as far as is possible, to convey to others the indescribable gifts that come to us in receptive prayer. Rufus Jones rightly points out that each man of prayer inevitably has to clothe in the thought-forms and presuppositions of his own age whatever he may receive. So if we are going to gain from these writings, whether from Père de Caussade, from John Cassian or from the apostle Paul, we need some very delicate translation, much more profound than merely linguistic translation.

Rufus Jones makes also quite a different, I think useful, distinction between negative mysticism and positive mysticism. He writes appreciatively of both types of mystics. In their writings on mystical theology – though probably it was not so in the prayer experience itself – some authors in an unbalanced way write of God in negative abstract terms. We saw that the author of *The Cloud* did so. These writers also sound rather negative too in their attitude to human nature and human feelings. Rufus Jones sees much of this negative mysticism stemming from Dionysius the Areopagite and so regards his widespread influence as unfortunate, but I am not sure that he is always quite fair to Dionysius.

On the other hand Rufus Jones writes about positive mysticism which emphasizes the closeness of God to us and the essential goodness of human nature. He grants that in all spiritual writers there is a mixture in varying proportions of negative and positive elements. He claims the stream of positive mysticism runs through Paul, John, Francis of Assisi, Jakob Boehme the Lutheran, Henry Vaughan, and then George Fox and his followers in the true Quaker tradition. There is, I think, in Rufus Jones a little special pleading and he may be more influenced than he realizes by his early twentieth-century, over-optimistic liberal presuppositions.

Further, he makes another distinctive contribution, when he recommends us sometimes to share together our time of silent receptive prayer with a small group of our friends. This may bring in a new dimension. It has hardly been hinted at by our other authors. Rufus Jones is speaking out of a lifetime of predominantly silent Quaker meetings. I have Quaker relatives and I would agree with him from my own experience in their deeper, or as they say 'gathered', meetings. I have had similar experiences in France when I have lived with the fraternities of the Little Brothers, inspired by Charles de Foucauld, and shared in their evening hour of silent adoration.

But what rings out most strongly from all his books – and he managed to write fifty-four – and from his own closely-packed eighty-five years are his words:

Those who would see God must gird themselves for service.

13

Bede Griffiths and our Small Earth

Had I been writing before the Second World War, I could have finished our survey with Rufus Jones. That is now impossible. Through jet planes, student travel, tourism, immigration and television we are on the doorstep of the East. People, old and young, are asking, 'How can the East help us in our Western "wasteland"?' A student of mine, for example, hitch-hiked from Oxford to Nepal to find a guru. So many are putting this question to me seriously, that I have recently re-visited the East. Among those I spoke to – Hindus, Buddhists, Moslems, Christians – I was particularly struck by Dom Bede Griffiths at his ashram in South India.

We drove west from old Trichinopoly along a fairly good road for India, lined by swaying palms and by gnarled trunks of tamarinds, with monkeys scuttling amongst the branches. On our left were banana plantations and paddyfields with every vivid tint of green. On our right was the slow-moving Cauvery river, almost a mile wide, 'the holy Ganges of South India'. We passed through a string of villages, crowded with children and grown-ups, each village with its small Hindu temple, often with figures of gods and goddesses in brilliant reds and blues and golds.

After about twenty miles we turned right up a short lane. And there we were, with Bede Griffiths waiting to welcome us – saffron-robed and barefoot. His calm face appealed to me, his flowing beard, with his hair falling to his shoulders – and his quiet, very agreeable voice. At once I was at ease with him. We sat and talked leisurely – there is leisure in India – in a bamboo grove leading down to the placid holy river. There was sparkling water also in an acre of paddyfield, with the ashram's own rice just sprouting up. I noticed their half-a-dozen cows, obviously well cared for – so different from the sad-eyed scavenging cows you see in every Indian village and town. The chapel of the ashram looked like a village temple, except that its figures were of Jesus and the saints; and in their services I was soon to feel a truly contemplative atmosphere with quiet Indian music and with slow Indian gestures of worship.

The place is rightly named Shantivanam – 'house of peace'. Father Bede has come here at the end of his long, fascinating, spiritual journey. And who are with him? Ten other monks, all Indians; and in their few simple guest-rooms Sisters and others seeking worship rooted in the soil of India; a few Hindus and rather more enquirers from the West, seeking prayer in depth.

For Bede, as for so many of us, 'the child is the father of the man'. He was at the well-known school, Christ's Hospital. Already he thought of entering the Indian Civil Service. In his final year he lost the Christian faith he had received in his home. But on an unforgettable evening in his last term he went for a walk alone. The hawthorn trees were in full bloom; there was the chorus of the birds at sunset; a feeling of awe came over him – and a new, inner, mysterious world opened up with what Wordsworth calls 'the glory and freshness of a dream'. Henry Vaughan knew such experiences – and I have too. For half-a-dozen years this nature-mysticism was to be Bede's religion, including his time as a student at Oxford. There he studied English literature under that skilled writer, C. S. Lewis. At that time they were both agnostics.

After taking a good degree in 1928, he with two other Oxford men set up in a Cotswold village a kind of a 'commune'. They were, as early as the thirties, looking for a simpler 'life-style': no car, no newspapers, no radio – TV of course was undreamed of – and no travelling by bus or by train. When Bede visited his mother he walked – seventy miles there and seventy back. On one of his visits he met a theosophist. She publicly smoked cigarettes in the street – a daring thing for a woman in those days. But more important, she introduced Bede to the *Bhagavad Gita* and to the Buddha's *Way of Virtue*.

In their cottage these three friends widened their literary studies, still directed by C. S. Lewis, who became a lifelong friend to Bede. They read – merely as literature – Augustine's *Confessions* 'in Latin of course', Lewis added in an aside; Dante, in Italian; Henry Vaughan and the seventeenth-century poets; and again, purely as seventeenth-century prose, the Authorized Version of the Bible. But then, as Bede was reading about Jesus in Mark's gospel, he felt inwardly compelled to kneel on the bare stone floor of the cottage –

and prayed for the first time since he was at school. His commitment to Jesus grew quickly. He began to think about the possibility of ordination, much to his mother's delight.

But he was recommended first to do a spell of work in the East end of London. It was a great strain for him. These were the years of the great slump. He was practising his religion in a very tense way. Once he prayed all through a night. As he got up from his knees, he seemed to hear a voice: 'You must go to a retreat.' But what was a retreat? – he didn't know. So he went at once to ask a priest, who explained and told Bede that one was starting that same evening at a retreat-house in Westminster. Bede went. The addresses were basic and spoke directly to his mind and heart. He felt moved to make his first confession. A burden was lifted from his shoulders. When he returned from the chapel to his room, his Bible was open at the words in the first letter of John: 'Herein is love, not that we loved God, but that he loved us and sent his Son.' Bede had been seeking God; but now God in his never-changing love had found him. It was a revelation of love. Bede had known affection in his family, he had many friends, he loved nature, he loved poetry. But now – let me quote his own words –

I felt that love had taken possession of my soul. It was as though a wave of love flowed over me, a love as real and personal as any human love could be and yet infinitely transcending all human limitations.[1]

When Bede came away from that retreat-house, all looked clear and settled. He went back to the Cotswolds, but now to live, wisely or unwisely, as a hermit. He was deep in the mystics, Christian, Hindu and Buddhist. He was soon in confusion, near to a nervous breakdown. But he was befriended by a shepherd and his family, and then worked on a farm.

At this time he had, I think, his only serious friendship with a girl, a South African. This is the kind of man he was and is. They went for long walks; they received communion together in the village church. She returned to South Africa and married, but they continued to write regularly, until she was killed by a fall from her horse. But in this way he discovered, so he says, that a true friendship, founded on the love of God, unites us so deeply that not even death can divide us.

Another book came into his hands, Newman's *Development of Christian Doctrine*, which led him to visit Prinknash, the Roman

Catholic Benedictine Priory, then in a charming old Cotswold manor house. I can see it now, looking down the valley of the Severn, with the magnificent tower of Gloucester cathedral, itself a Benedictine Abbey in the Middle Ages. At once Bede felt at home with these monks and their life of worship and he discovered his vocation. Already, as we have seen, he had read a good deal of Christian literature in a random way. But now it fell into a pattern in his monastic study of the Catholic faith. Afterwards he was allowed to return to the Hindu and Buddhist classics. No longer did they disrupt his life of prayer, nor did they lead him to superficial religious synthesis; in fact they deepened his Catholic prayer.

After being entrusted with several responsible posts in his community, he was allowed to go to India. He first helped to found a monastery in a very simple Indian style, high up in the Western Ghats in Kerala, where I was sixteen years ago. Once that monastery was well established, he went with two monks and took over his present ashram. It had been founded by two French priests who have died in recent years, Père Monchanin and Père le Saux, who took the name Abhishiktananda and whose small book, simply entitled *Prayer*, has opened doors for many people.

I found I had much in common with Bede Griffiths, including an admiration for that Roman Catholic lay theologian, Baron von Hügel, who is relevant to the inter-faith dialogue about prayer. Von Hügel insists that a balanced religion needs three elements – the intellectual, the corporate and the mystical. Bede Griffiths thinks that western Christianity has over-emphasized the intellectual and corporate, and underplayed the mystical.

In our chapter on Rufus Jones we had some difficulty with this word 'mystical'; I think we could substitute for it 'contemplative', in a wide sense, or even 'existential' or 'personal'. Contact with Hindus, or at least their sannayasis, could help us Westerners to redress this balance. Bede Griffiths and many in India are convinced about this. These eastern holy men ask not so much 'What do you think about God?' as 'How have you experienced God?' They and Christian men and women of prayer find they understand one another when they speak of the stages of their spiritual journey, and even of the summit they all approach. This dialogue has already enriched Bede Griffiths' own life of prayer and he believes that it will do so more and more for him and for others. Thomas Merton the Trappist said the same during his own journey in the East. The

Hindu claims that he is approaching Brahman, the Eternal Being; the Buddhist, Nirvana, the passing away of the relative and the temporal; and the Christian claims to be met by the Logos, the Word of God, the Love of God disclosed. The Logos, so the Christian believes, is the Light, who enlightens every man who genuinely seeks – Hindu, Buddhist, Christian or whatever he may be – whether he recognizes this or not. So Bede Griffiths declares, 'The mystery of Christ is present in all religions, in an embryonic form,'[2] while he still firmly maintains that we do not seek for some synthesis of these different faiths.

Patiently and closely as he approaches the Hindus, Bede holds firmly to his conviction that, although God discloses himself to seekers of other faiths, there is something unique in God's disclosure in Christ. This is, as we have seen, the faith of the New Testament. But the Hindus themselves as yet find it impossible to acknowledge in any sense the unparalleledness of Jesus. This dialogue I am convinced must go on – and especially in ashrams, Hindu and Christian.

Even those of us who are little more than beginners in Christian prayer can learn something from the East – and in particular that prayer is not just a mental exercise. Prayer involves the whole personality, body and feelings, as well as the intellect. What the Easterners say about posture and breathing exercises may help some of us towards deeper prayer. Middle-aged Westerners, it is true, are not very flexible, especially about the knees. Ignatius Loyola wrote about postures for prayer, about kneeling, sitting and prostrating; and he specially recommended us to stand still for a few moments, considering what a wonderful thing it is to be able to pray, before we actually kneel or sit for prayer.

More important is the emphasis which the Easterners put on the need of a guru. Some of us may have been a bit put off by what we've been told about heavy-handed methods of some eastern gurus and of some Zen masters. But Bede Griffiths assured me that the best gurus are as perceptive and sensitive as Francis de Sales. And certainly all Christians should know the words of one of our finest sixteenth-century guides, Father Augustine Baker: 'The spiritual guide is not to teach his own way, but to instruct others how they may find out the way proper to them.'

What impressed me also is how seriously many of the Easterners take the discipline of their life of prayer. In transcendental meditation, which is a modification of Hindu meditation designed for people of any or of no faith, even beginners, whatever their age, are required to make two periods of twenty minutes of meditation every day, without fail.

If we wish to be close to a friend, we make time, don't we – to meet, or at least to write? And if we want real fellowship with God through prayer, we too in the West will each need to look at, or look again at, our lives and see what time we can find – and safeguard. We have often seen in this book how the life of prayer needs sustained effort. But I am not going to suggest a rigid rule; so don't be alarmed. Francis de Sales, when he drew up guidelines for himself, qualified them by adding, 'And love is my rule'. But to help you to plan a few clear guidelines for yourself, perhaps with the advice of a guide who knows you, let me say what I try to do and why.

For me half-a-dozen simple things are important. What I discover matters most of all is a regular, if possible daily, time for meditation or for that quieter, more receptive prayer that grows out of it. Every morning I think of Jesus finding a quiet place early in the day. I am freshest then. A different hour may suit your life and energies better. Next I need time for what used to be called 'saying our prayers'. It might be some fresh way of talking with God – thanking him, saying we're sorry and praying for others and for ourselves. For me this comes before I go to bed or earlier in the evening.

Then I look for an opportunity, at least once a week, to think about the scriptures and the Christian faith. The more wordless my meditation may become, the more it should be balanced by reading and thinking. Rufus Jones was clear about that. Also I welcome the chance for some kind of praying together and talking together on a regular basis; for even the most independently minded of us, I think, require some mutual encouragement – and challenge. And the holy communion becomes for many of us the focus and heart of this praying together.

And lastly I know I need other, longer times for keeping fresh my prayer and commitment to the Lord. So a yearly retreat away from home or even a quiet day of prayer possibly in a local church becomes something to look forward to.

These ways of prayer, lovingly and steadily maintained, will, I hope, increasingly overflow into my ordinary life and bring me nearer to the 'praying without ceasing' of Paul and the Desert Fathers – to that openness by means of which the present moment becomes a sacrament.

All this planning is not just to help ourselves; because our primary purpose, as the New Testament and John Cassian remind us, is our collaboration with God, by prayer, by love and by action, for the coming of his kingdom. 'For without God,' Augustine says, 'we cannot, and without us God will not.'

Yet we may sometimes feel drawn also to read the spiritual treasures of other faiths. I am an amateur in this field, but I am thinking of some gems of the Sufis, the Moslem mystics. But fundamentally – and Jung says this on psychological grounds – I think we are wise to ground ourselves in our own Christian tradition. Even when we English try to speak in French and German, we usually say our personal prayers in English. Yet John Dunne, the American Jesuit, in his book, *The Way of All the Earth*,[3] says that some of us from the western wasteland almost have to travel East – in body or in mind – to have our spiritual eyes opened; then on our return we can appreciate the treasures of our western contemplative tradition.

You may know a Latin poem which, in translation, asks, 'But what to those who find?' – those who find this deep fellowship with God in love and prayer. It says neither lips nor pen can express it; and only those who love actually know. Father Bede, and those other writers, we sense, have really 'found'. And they are men and women like ourselves – so we too can 'find', if we set out with considered guidelines and joyful expectancy.

Notes

Chapter 1. John Cassian and the Desert

1. T. Roszak, *Where the Wasteland Ends*, Doubleday, NY 1973, p. 394.
2. Igumen Chariton, *The Art of Prayer*, Faber 1966, p. 268.

Chapter 2. Psalmists and being Ourselves

1. Thomas Merton, *Bread in the Wilderness*, Hollis & Carter 1954, p. 45.
2. Dietrich Bonhoeffer, *Letters and Papers from Prison*, The Enlarged Edition, SCM Press 1971, p. 40.
3. G. B. Hume, *Searching for God*, Hodder & Stoughton 1977, p. 51.
4. H. P. van Dusen, *Dag Hammarskjöld*, Faber 1967, p. 139.
5. Harvey Guthrie, *Israel's Sacred Songs*, Seabury Press, NY 1966, p. 204.

Chapter 3. Jesus and Abba

1. C. H. Dodd, *The Founder of Christianity*, Collins Fount 1971, p. 33.
2. Joachim Jeremias, *The Central Message of the New Testament*, SCM Press 1965, p. 21.
3. Dodd, op. cit., p. 63.
4. Jeremias, op. cit., p. 28.
6. René Voillaume, *Seeds of the Desert*, Burns & Oates 1955, p. 184.

Chapter 4. Paul and the Spirit

1. F. Heiler, *Prayer*, OUP 1932, p. iv.
2. René Voillaume, *Au Coeur des Masses*, part 3, ch. 1, *Petits Frères de Jésus*, Editions du Cerf, Paris 1950, p. 176.

Chapter 5. John and God's Love

1. Leon Morris, *St John's Gospel*, Marshall, Morgan & Scott 1971, p. 7.
2. Rudolf Bultmann, *The Gospel of John*, Blackwell 1971, p. 5.
3. A. M. Ramsey, *The Glory of God and the Transfiguration of Christ*, Longmans 1949, p. 89.
4. R. E. Brown, *The Gospel according to St John*, Anchor Bible, Chapman 1972, vol. ii. p. 582.
5. William Temple, *Readings in St John's Gospel*, Macmillan 1939, p. 6.

Chapter 7. Ignatius Loyola and Teresa of Avila

1. J. Broderick, *Origin of the Jesuits*, Longmans 1940, p. 1.
2. This was unknown even to the Jesuits until 1892. Probably the best edition with a sensitive introduction is St Ignace, *Journal Spirituel*, translated into French by M. Giuliani, Desclée de Brouwer, Paris 1958. There is, as far as I know, no English edition.
3. A list of retreats is published annually in *Vision*, Association for Promoting Retreats, Church House, Newton Road, London W2 5LS.

Chapter 11. Jean-Pierre de Caussade and the Present Moment

1. L. Martz, *The Poetry of Meditation*, Yale University Press 1962, p. 50.

Chapter 12. Rufus Jones and Today's World

1. In R. M. Jones, *The Radiant Life*, Macmillan & Co., NY 1944, p. 96.

Chapter 13. Bede Griffiths and our Small Earth

1. Bede Griffiths, *The Golden String*, Harvill Press 1954, p. 97.
2. Bede Griffiths, *Christian Ashram*, Darton, Longman & Todd 1966, p. 188.
3. Sheldon Press 1973.

For Further Reading

Chapter 1. John Cassian and the Desert

H. Chadwick, *The Early Church*, Penguin 1967
  Particularly ch. 12, 'The Ascetic Movement'.
W. O. Chadwick, *John Cassian*, CUP, 2nd edition 1968
D. Knowles, *Christian Monasticism*, Weidenfeld & Nicholson 1969
  A perceptive survey of the influence of the monks through the centuries.
Thomas Merton, *Wisdom of the Desert*, Hollis & Carter 1961
Sister Benedicta Ward, *The Wisdom of the Desert Fathers*, SLG Press, Oxford
  1975

Chapter 2. Psalmists and being Ourselves

The Psalms, A New Translation, Collins Fount 1975
  This version is based on the Hebrew text, but the psalms are numbered from
  the Greek text. The adjustment is easily made, as is explained in the preface.
  The singing version of this book has a short introduction to each psalm. Most
  of my quotations are from this edition.
P. R. Ackroyd, *Doors of Perception: A Guide to Reading the Psalms*, Faith Press
  1978
J. H. Eaton, *Psalms*, Torch Commentary, SCM Press 1967
Thomas Merton, *On the Psalms*, Sheldon Press 1977
H. H. Rowley, *Worship in Ancient Israel*, SPCK 1967

Chapter 3. Jesus and Abba

Gunther Bornkamm, *Jesus of Nazareth*, Hodder & Stoughton 1960
Thomas Corbishley, *The Prayer of Jesus*, Mowbrays 1976
C. H. Dodd, *The Founder of Christianity*, Collins 1971; Collins Fount 1973
Joachim Jeremias, *The Central Message of the New Testament*, SCM Press 1965
Joachim Jeremias, *The Prayers of Jesus*, SCM Press 1967

Chapter 4. Paul and the Spirit

A. Vidler and M. Muggeridge, *Paul: Envoy Extraordinary*, Collins 1972
J. B. Phillips, *Letters to Young Churches*, Collins Fount 1955

A free translation of the epistles with a few notes. (These two books would make a good first introduction for the beginner.)

William Barclay, *The Mind of St Paul*, Collins 1958; Collins Fount 1965

Gunther Bornkamm, *Paul*, Hodder & Stoughton 1969
One of the best recent books linking his letters and his theology.

Donald Coggan, *Prayers of the New Testament*, Hodder & Stoughton 1967
Includes a study of Paul's prayers in his letters.

A. C. Deane, *St Paul and his Letters*, Hodder & Stoughton 1942
Clear and non-technical.

J. S. Stewart, *Man in Christ*, Hodder & Stoughton 1935; reissued 1972
Has a good section on Paul's spirituality.

Chapter 5. *John and God's Love*

George Appleton, *John's Witness to Jesus*, Lutterworth 1955
An admirable lead-in to John.

Barnabas Lindars, *John*, Oliphants 1972
A substantial modern commentary.

Alan Richardson, *Saint John*, Torch Commentary, SCM Press 1959
A useful commentary for beginners.

William Temple, *Readings in St John's Gospel*, Macmillan 1939
A series of meditations.

Chapter 6. *Mother Julian and* The Cloud of Unknowing

Julian of Norwich, *Revelations of Divine Love*, Penguin 1966

The Cloud of Unknowing, Penguin 1961
Both translated by Clifton Wolters from medieval into contemporary English, with excellent introductions.

W. Johnston, *The Still Point*, Harper & Row 1971
Reflections on Zen and Christian Mysticism, including *The Cloud of Unknowing*.

D. Knowles, *The English Mystical Tradition*, Burns & Oates 1961

P. Molinari, *Julian of Norwich*, Longmans 1958
A scholarly study.

Chapter 7. *Ignatius Loyola and Teresa of Avila*

J. Broderick, *St Ignatius Loyola: Pilgrim Years*, Burns & Oates 1956

J. F. O'Callaghan, *Autobiography of St Ignatius Loyola*, Harper & Row 1974
A short account related in his last years to his secretary.

T. Corbishley (ed), *Spiritual Exercises of St Ignatius Loyola*, Anthony Clarke 1973

L. von Matt and H. Rahner, *St Ignatius of Loyola*, Longmans 1956
A short biography remarkably illustrated.

E. Hamilton, *Servants of Love*, Darton, Longman & Todd 1975
A useful 100-page introduction to Teresa of Avila.

E. Allison Peers, *Complete Works of St Teresa* (three volumes) Sheed and Ward 1946

E. Allison Peers, *Mother of Carmel*, SCM Press 1945; reissued 1979
A portrait of St Teresa of Jesus.

G. Brenan, *St John of the Cross, his Life and Poetry*, CUP 1976

E. Hamilton, *The Voice of the Spirit*, Darton, Longman & Todd 1976
A short introduction to John of the Cross.

E. Allison Peers, *Spirit of Flame*, SCM Press 1943; reissued 1979
A study of St John of the Cross.

Chapter 8. Francis de Sales and Jeanne de Chantal

M. de la Bedoyere, *Francis de Sales*, Collins 1960

Francis de Sales, *Introduction to the Devout Life*, Burns & Oates 1930

Francis de Sales, *Treatise on the Love of God* (ed H. B. Mackey), Burns & Oates 1930

Francis de Sales, *Spiritual Letters* (ed E. Stopp), Faber 1960

E. Stopp, *Mme de Chantal*, Faber 1962
These last two books are probably the best account in English.

Chapter 9. Vincent de Paul and Louise de Marillac

P. Coste, *Life and Works of Vincent de Paul* (three volumes), Burns & Oates 1935

J. Leonard, *Vincent de Paul and Mental Prayer*, Burns & Oates 1925

M. Purcell, *The World of M. Vincent*, Harvill Press 1963

M. V. Woodgate, *Vincent de Paul*, Brown & Nolan, Dublin 1958

Louise de Marillac, *Letters*, St Joseph's House Press, Maryland 1972

J. I. Dirvin, *Louise de Marillac*, Farrar, Straus and Giroux, NY 1970

M. V. Woodgate, *Louise de Marillac*, Brown & Nolan, Dublin 1942

Chapter 10. Henry Vaughan and Awareness

Henry Vaughan, *Complete Poems* (ed A. Rudrum), Penguin 1976

Henry Vaughan, *Selected Poems* (ed with an introduction by R. B. Shaw), Carcanet Press 1976
A useful introduction.

J. Bennett, *Five Metaphysical Poets*, CUP 1964

H. Bremond, *Prayer and Poetry*, Burns & Oates 1927

Helen Gardner (ed) *The Metaphysical Poets*, Penguin 1972
A general introduction and seventeen of Vaughan's poems.

F. E. Hutchinson, *Henry Vaughan*, OUP 1947
The standard biography.

Chapter 11. Jean-Pierre de Caussade and the Present Moment

Jean-Pierre de Caussade, *Self-Abandonment to Divine Providence*, Collins Fount 1971

Jean-Pierre de Caussade, *Lettres Spirituelles* (ed M.-O. Gaillard), Desclée de Brouwer, Paris 1964 (two volumes)

Chapter 12. Rufus Jones and Today's World

H. E. Fosdick (ed), *Rufus Jones Speaks to Our Time*, Bannisdale Press 1953

An excellent anthology, now obtainable from The Book Centre, Friends' House, Euston Road, London NW1.

E. G. Vining, *Friend of Life*, Michael Joseph 1959

The standard biography.

Chapter 13. Bede Griffiths and our Small Earth

Bede Griffiths, *Christian Ashram*, Darton, Longman & Todd 1966

Bede Griffiths, *The Golden String*, Harvill Press 1954

Autobiography up to his becoming a Benedictine.

Bede Griffiths, *Return to the Centre*, Collins Fount 1978

Abhishiktananda (Henri Le Saux), *Prayer*, SPCK 1972